Applying Psychology in the Classroom

Jane Leadbetter, Sue Morris, Gren Knight, Paul Timmins and Dave Traxson

David Fulton Publishers
London

David Fulton Publishers Ltd
Ormond House, 26–27 Boswell Street, London WC1N 3JD

First published in Great Britain by David Fulton Publishers 1999

British Library Cataloguing in Publication Data
A catalogue record for this book is available from the British Library.

ISBN 1–85346–584–4

Typeset by Saxon Graphics Ltd, Derby.
Printed in Great Britain by The Cromwell Press Ltd, Trowbridge, Wilts.

Contents

Contributors

Jane Leadbetter is a Senior Educational Psychologist for Birmingham LEA and is involved in advising, supporting and training teachers, particularly in the area of behaviour management. She works at the School of Education, University of Birmingham as part of the Educational Psychology team and is currently researching effective practice between educational psychologists and schools.

Sue Morris is the Director of Professional Training in Educational Psychology at the University of Birmingham and continues to practise as an educational psychologist. Her particular interests include the mental health of both children and adolescents and the central role which schools and families can play in supporting children's psychological well-being, personal growth and educational achievements.

Paul Timmins is a Professional and Academic tutor to the training course in educational psychology at the University of Birmingham. He also works as a Senior Educational Psychologist in Solihull LEA. He was recently awarded his doctorate for work on the role of the SENCo and school improvement and his other interests include research processes which stimulate improvement as well as group processes and learning for both adults and pupils.

Gren Knight is a Senior Educational Psychologist in Wolverhampton and also an Academic and Professional tutor to the Educational Psychology training course at the University of Birmingham. He has a particular interest in the application of organisational psychology within education and has undertaken research on the effects of school furniture on behaviour and learning. Other interests include children with emotional and behaviour difficulties and those with severe learning difficulties.

Dave Traxson is a Senior Educational Psychologist in Wolverhampton and was an Academic and Professional tutor at the University of Birmingham for five years until July 1998. He has interests in cognitive behavioural psychology, humanistic psychology, innovative methods of counselling and supporting children to be more self-directing in their behaviour.

Foreword

Each publication in this series of books is concerned with approaches to intervention with children with specific needs in mainstream schools. In this preface we provide a backdrop of general issues concerning special needs in mainstream schools. The government's recent Action Programme, published after considering responses to the Special Educational Needs (SEN) Green Paper, will lead to changes in practice in the future. Following consultation, there will be a revised and simplified Code of Practice in place by the school year 2000/2001. It is intended that this will make life easier.

The SEN Code of Practice (DfE 1994a), following the 1993 Education Act, provides practical guidance to LEAs and school governing bodies on their responsibilities towards pupils with SEN. Schools and LEAs were required to regard its recommendations from September 1994. The Department for Education also issued Circular 6/94 (DfE 1994b) which provided suggestions as to how schools should manage their special needs provision alongside that made by other local schools. These documents embody the twin strategies of individual pupil support and whole-school development. The Green Paper *Excellence for All* also seeks to promote the development of more sophisticated and comprehensive forms of regional and local planning (DfEE 1997).

The Code of Practice, with its staged approach to assessment supervised within each mainstream school by a teacher designated as Special Educational Needs Coordinator (SENCO), was widely welcomed.

For example, Walters (1994) argued that 'this Code of Practice builds on good practice developed over the ten years and heralds a "new deal" for children with special needs in the schools of England and Wales'. But he also reflected worries that, in the light of other developments, the process might provide an added incentive for schools to dump their 'problem children into the lap of the LEA' rather than devising strategies to improve behaviour in the school environment. Such children, he feared, were in danger of being increasingly marginalised.

Impact on teachers

While receiving a mainly positive welcome for its intentions, the Code of Practice (DfE 1994a) also raised some concerns about its impact on teachers who became responsible for its implementation. On the positive side the Code would raise the profile of special needs and establish a continuum of provision in mainstream schools. There was a clear specification of different types of special educational need and the Code's emphasis was on meeting them through individual programmes developed in cooperation with parents.

However, there were possible problems in meeting the challenge of establishing effective and time-efficient procedures for assessment and monitoring. Further challenges were to be found in making best use of resources and overcoming barriers to liaison with parents.

Anxieties about the Code

Following the introduction of the Code these anxieties were confirmed by a number of research studies of teachers' perceptions of the impact of the Code. The picture which emerged from these studies showed appreciation of the potential benefits of implementing the Code but widespread anxiety, based on early experience, about the practicalities of making it work.

Loxley and Bines (1995) interviewed head teachers and SENCOs about their views on emergent issues related to the complexities of introducing Individual Education Plans (IEPs), particularly in secondary schools.

Teachers feared that 'excessive proceduralism' could lead to the distribution of resources being skewed towards meeting the needs of children whose parents are best able to understand and exercise their rights, at the expense of provision for children whose parents are less assertive and confident. Teachers were most concerned about the allocation of scarce resources and the increased responsibilities of SENCOs for managing a system likely to reduce time for direct teaching of children.

School perspectives

Most schools were optimistic about their ability to implement the Code and positive about LEA guidelines and training, but there was less certainty that the Code would improve the education of pupils with SEN.

Asked to give their opinion on advantages and disadvantages of the Code, teachers cited as positive effects:

- a more structured framework,
- growing awareness of accountability,
- a higher profile for SEN issues,
- earlier identification,
- greater uniformity in practice, and
- increased parental involvement.

The disadvantages cited were:

- lack of resources and time,
- substantially increased workloads for all teachers as well as SENCOs,
- more time used for liaison and less for teaching.

(Rhodes, 1996)

Four themes

A national survey commissioned by the National Union of Teachers (NUT) identified four themes:

1. broad support for the principles and establishment of the Code of Practice;
2. concern about the feasibility of its implementation, given a lack of time and resources;
3. problems in some areas related to perceived inadequacy of LEA support;
4. inadequate status and lack of recognition for the SENCO role.

(Lewis *et al.*, 1996)

Another study found patchy support for SENCOs. There were wide variations in the amount of time dedicated to the role, the amount of support from head teachers and governors, involvement in decision-making, the extent of training and the degree of bureaucracy within LEAs.

SEN Register and Staged Assessment Procedures

Although its widespread adoption makes it appear to have been a national prescription, the five-stage model suggested in the Code is not a legal requirement. The Code actually states that: 'to give specific help to children who have special educational needs, schools should adopt a staged response'. (DfE 1994a, 2.20)

It goes on to indicate that some schools and LEAs may adopt different models but that, while it was not essential that there should be five stages, it was essential that there should be differentiation between the stages, aimed at matching action taken to the pupil's needs at each stage.

Five Key Stages

Nonetheless, the normal expectation is that assessment and intervention will be organised and recorded in an SEN Register for which the SENCO is responsible. The following description briefly summarises usual practice, with Stages 1–3 school-based and Stages 4 and 5 the responsibility of the LEA.

Stage 1
Class teacher identifies pupils with learning difficulty and, with support from the SENCO, attempts to meet the pupil's SEN.

Stage 2
Class teacher reports continued concern and SENCO takes responsibility for the special response to meet the pupil's SEN.

Stage 3
SENCO organises support from external agencies to help in meeting the pupil's SEN.

Stage 4
The LEA is approached by the school with a request for statutory assessment.

Stage 5
The LEA considers the need for a Statement of SEN and completes the assessment procedure; monitoring and review of the statement is organised by the LEA.

Each book in this series explains how this process works in relation to different disabilities and difficulties as they were described in the 1981 Act and shows how individual needs can be identified and met through IEPs. While forthcoming revision of the Code may alter the details of the stages, the principles of the practices through which needs are specified will remain the same.

Information for colleagues, governors and parents

Ensuring that the school provides all necessary information for staff, governors and parents is another major element of the SENCO role. *The Organisation of Special Educational Provision* (Circular 6/94) (DfE 1994b) sets out the issues which the school should address about its SEN provision, policies and partnerships with bodies beyond the school.

This is information that must be made available and may be found in school brochures or prospectuses, in annual reports to parents and in policy documents. The ultimate responsibility for following the guidance in the Circular rests with the head teacher and governing body but the SENCO will be engaged with all these issues. Effectively, the Circular forms a useful checklist for monitoring the development and implementation of the SEN policy.

You may find it useful to consider the following points as a way of familiarising yourself with provision in your school.

Basic information about your school's special educational provision

- Who is responsible for coordinating the day-to-day provision of education for pupils with SEN at your school (whether or not the person is known as the SEN Coordinator)?
- Arrangements need to be made for coordinating the provision of education for pupils with SEN. Does your school's SENCO work alone or is there a coordinating or support team?
- What are the admission arrangements for pupils with SEN who do not have a statement and is there any priority for SEN admissions ?
- What kind of provision does your school have for the special educational needs in which it specialises?
- What are your school's access arrangements for pupils with physical and sensory disabilities?

Information about the school's policies for the identification, assessment and provision for all pupils with SEN

- What is your school policy on allocation of money for SEN resources?
- How are pupils with SEN identified and their needs determined and reviewed? How are parents told about this?

- What does your school policy say about arrangements for providing access for pupils with SEN to a balanced and broadly-based curriculum (including the National Curriculum)?
- What does your school policy say about 'integration arrangements'? How do pupils with SEN engage in the activities of the school together with pupils who do not have special educational needs?
- How does your school demonstrate the effective implementation of its SEN policy? How does the governing body evaluate the success of the education which is provided at the school for pupils with SEN?
- What are the arrangements made by the governing body relating to the treatment of complaints from parents of pupils with SEN concerning the provision made at the school?
- What are your school's 'time targets' for response to complaints?

Information about the school's staffing policies and partnership with bodies beyond the school

- What is your school's policy on continuing in-service professional training for staff in relation to special educational needs?
- What are your school's arrangements regarding the use of teachers and facilities from outside the school, including links with support services for special educational needs?
- What is the role played by the parents of pupils with SEN? Is there a 'close working relationship'?
- Do you have any links with other schools, including special schools, and is there provision made for the transition of pupils with SEN between schools or between the school and the next stage of life or education?
- How well does 'liaison and information exchange' work in your school, e.g. links with health services, social services and educational welfare services and any voluntary organisations which work on behalf of children with SEN?

In any school those arrangements which are generally available to meet children's learning needs will have an impact on those services which are required to meet specific needs. It is therefore very important that a reader of any one of this series of specialist books makes reference to the general situation in their school when thinking about ways of improving the learning situation for pupils.

Harry Daniels and Colin Smith
The University of Birmingham
February 1999

References

Crowther, D., Dyson, A. *et al.* (1997) *Implementation of the Code of Practice: The Role of the Special Educational Needs Coordinator*. Special Needs Research Centre, Department of Education, University of Newcastle upon Tyne.

Department for Education (DfE) (1994a) *Code of Practice on the Identification and Assessment of Special Educational Needs*. London: HMSO.

Department for Education (DfE) (1994b) *The Organisation of Special Educational Provision*. Circular 6/94. London: HMSO.

Department for Education and Employment (DfEE) (1997) *Excellence for All: Meeting Special Educational Needs*. London: HMSO.

Hornby, G. (1995) 'The Code of Practice: boon or burden', *British Journal of Special Education* **22**(3) 116–119.

Lewis, A., Neill, S. R. St J. and Campbell, R. J. (1996) *The Implementation of the Code of Practice in Primary and Secondary School: A National Survey of the Perceptions of Special Educational Needs Coordinators*. The University of Warwick.

Loxley, A. and Bines, H. (1995) 'Implementing the Code of Practice: professional responses', *Support for Learning* **10**(4) 185–189.

Rhodes, L. W. (1996) *'Code of Practice: first impressions'*, *Special!* Spring 1996.

Walters, B. (1994) *Management of Special Needs*. London: Cassell.

Introduction

Paul Timmins

Audience and orientation

This book is written primarily for newly qualified primary teachers and any teachers interested in the application of psychologically based approaches in the classroom. Its orientation is eclectic, drawing on a variety of psychological theories we have found useful in our work as educational psychologists in schools. It is psychological in the sense that it is concerned with the science of the mind, particularly as this relates to the way in which teachers and pupils think about life and work in the classroom. It also introduces ways in which teachers can influence classroom culture and climate in order to ensure that all pupils learn effectively and develop a strong sense of self-esteem, whatever their level of ability.

This book does not claim to be a preparation for teaching. Issues such as curriculum planning and review and theories which inform teaching and learning are dealt with admirably elsewhere, e.g. Desforges 1995, Cohen *et al.* 1996 and Pollard 1996. However, we share some of the important values and perspectives promoted in these works and we anticipate that those reading this book have a similar orientation. These include the following qualities which we believe to be characteristic of the effective and reflective teacher:

- A curiosity about the impact of teaching on pupils at the level of feelings and confidence as well as in terms of more academic outcomes and a need to engage pupils in discussion of these issues on a regular basis. Through this process pupils will come to understand how teachers attempt to support their learning and teachers will understand whether or not they have been successful in their efforts.
- An inclusive orientation to their teaching and a belief that it is possible to acquire the professional and personal skills necessary to meet a wide range of pupil needs in their classroom.

The content and orientation of the book are consistent with the implications of the Code of Practice for Special Educational Needs DfE 1994. These guidelines are predicated on the notion that some 20 per cent of pupils in mainstream schools will require teachers to conduct a careful and sympathetic analysis of their teaching and learning needs at some stage of their school life, in order to help them to overcome obstacles to learning. The perspectives on teaching and learning presented in the book enable teachers to recognise and deal with many of the difficulties pupils encounter in their learning either through attention to the management of the whole-class group or through more individualised approaches.

The Code identifies many difficulties which pupils may face in the classroom and requires that teachers formulate initial strategies to tackle these. They include emotional and behaviour difficulties, general learning difficulties and specific difficulties in acquiring literacy and/or numeracy skills. Whilst there are many excellent texts which present detailed strategies teachers might use to address these difficulties e.g. Cornwall and Tod 1998, McNamara and Moreton 1997, this book describes approaches not easily available to teachers in the education literature and which have proved popular in our in-service training with teachers (INSET) and casework with schools. The strategies and concepts we describe have provided teachers with insights which have enabled them to support individual pupils in their learning and to improve their classroom learning environments.

Teachers using the book will be enabled to extend their repertoire of teaching skills and by sharing these practices with other colleagues in school they will enhance their school's capacity to cater for a broad range of educational needs. Dyson 1990 and Ainscow 1991 suggest that all teachers should be helped to develop skills which enable them to overcome a range of blocks to learning likely to be experienced by pupils. Dyson, in particular, suggests that schools should attempt to identify these skills and encourage teachers to acquire them as part of the process of inclusion.

Stoll and Fink 1996 provide an account of how professional development activities for teachers can make a contribution to pupil achievement and therefore school improvement. Schools which give high priority to the development of teaching skills through professional development activities and have sensitive and supportive systems for ensuring that these are introduced to the classroom, help create vital conditions for school improvement as reflected in enhanced educational outcomes and pupils with confidence in their abilities as learners.

The content of this book

Chapter 1, 'The inclusive classroom', considers current developments in the education of children with special educational needs and in particular the move towards more inclusive education. Important differences between inclusion and integration are discussed and the implications of increasing inclusion for practising teachers are considered. The chapter suggests that effective special needs teaching should be based on sound principles underlying all teaching. An approach to working with all pupils is described. Finally, techniques and resources for supporting inclusion provide some ideas for next steps that can be tried in the classroom and school.

Chapter 2, 'Understanding the learning environment', describes two psychological approaches which are helpful for understanding and optimising the setting in which teaching and learning take place. The first perspective applies knowledge from 'Ergonomics' or 'Human Factors' psychology to the classroom. The focus of this section is on the interaction between people and the physical environment. The second perspective considers the psychosocial environment. It describes ways of assessing perceptions of how pupils and teachers feel they relate to each other and work together.

Chapter 3, '*Managing the social dynamics of the classroom*', underlines the relationship between social and academic development and builds on the notion that the quality of learning in the classroom is inextricably linked with prevailing social processes. It considers some of the steps which the class teacher can take to help ensure that the pupils in the class feel secure in their relationships, and that a collaborative working ethos is created and maintained.

Chapter 4, '*De-stressing children in the classroom*', aims to increase teachers' awareness of the part stress plays in triggering behavioural difficulties and learning problems in children. It offers ways of identifying these stresses and of helping to generate a positive cycle of success for all involved. It suggests a wide range of strategies for individual children or groups in order to ameliorate these effects.

Chapter 5, '*Exploring pupil motivation and promoting effective learning in the classroom*', describes approaches which can be used in the classroom to help teachers understand how pupils view what they are learning and whether or not they feel their efforts will be successful. These explorations help with an understanding of why pupils fail or lose their sense of motivation. The chapter also presents strategies which can be used with individuals and groups of pupils to improve their motivation and ability to cope with and learn from any frustrations and difficulties they associate with learning. Models for planning and reviewing teaching and learning are also presented. These can be used by adults and pupils alike to plan and review a wide range of activities both in and out of school.

Chapter 6, '*Conclusions: Using psychology as a basis for action*', reinforces themes which have been introduced in the book and suggests future developments which are likely to impact upon teachers' practice.

Using the book

We acknowledge some variations in presentational style between chapters and hope that these contribute in a positive manner to enrich the experience of reading and using the book. To a great extent, they match the mood and tenor of the topics introduced, and of course, the personal styles of enthusiasm of each author.

Each chapter in the book provides a particular perspective on an aspect of classroom life and to use the book effectively we would encourage teachers to adopt a reflective, experimental, 'suck it and see' stance towards approaches of particular interest. The planning, implementation and review process described below could be shared with a teacher colleague or used with a professional peer support group. The planning and review grid for the Self-Organised Learning approach described in Chapter 5 could also be used as an additional resource to support the process of implementation. We suggest the following steps:

- First, marshal aspirations for your classroom and your values as a teacher in relation to the themes suggested by the relevant chapter title.

- Then reflect on the strengths and weaknesses in your current day-to-day practice in relation to these and identify areas for development.
- Read the chapter selected and identify any fresh and useful perspectives in it, assimilate these within your value and practice frameworks and then identify any useful developments which you would like to make to present practice. (Each chapter contains questions which will help with reflection on current practice and may help with the identification of areas for further development.)
- Formulate an action plan to introduce these developments in a small-step and manageable way, with a clear purpose for the approach and sound awareness of its place in the development of pupils' knowledge and skills. Develop advance notions of how the strategy introduced is intended to impact on pupils and some way of measuring whether this actually happens in practice. Make a clear decision to carry out this evaluation and set a specific time and date for this.
- A review of progress made should be carried out with strategies being modified in the light of experience.

Further reading

Ainscow, M. (ed.) (1991) *Effective Schools For All*. London: David Fulton Publishers.

Clark, C., Dyson, A. and Millward, A. (eds) (1997) *New Directions in Special Needs: Innovations in Mainstream Schools*. London: Cassell.

Cohen, L., Manion, L. and Morris, K. (1996) *A Guide to Teaching Practice* (4th edn) London: Routledge.

Desforges, C. (1995) *An Introduction to Teaching: Psychological Perspectives*. Oxford: Blackwell.

Pollard, A. (ed.) (1996) *Readings for Reflective Teaching in the Primary School*. London: Cassell Education.

Stoll, L. and Fink, D. (1996) *Changing our Schools*. Buckingham: Open University Press.

CHAPTER 1

The inclusive classroom: taking account of the individual

Jane Leadbetter

Introduction

Within this book each chapter attempts to address current issues which are important for practising teachers and to consider how the use of psychological knowledge can improve their practice in the classroom. In this chapter, we consider current developments in the education of children with special educational needs and in particular the move towards more inclusive education. The approach taken is itself inclusive as it considers all children as individuals, rather than focusing upon children with special needs in particular, and looks at the skills which are necessary for teachers to become more effective with every individual in their class.

Effective teaching implies a reflective approach where practitioners scrutinise all aspects of their practice and aim to continuously improve on their previous best. In this area, more than any other, the beliefs, attitudes and values of practitioners play an important part in the success of individual children and so it is important that we reflect on our own attitudes in relation to children with special needs and appropriate education for them.

Inclusive education is a term which is becoming common parlance in educational circles and yet many teachers are confused about its meaning, its relevance to them and its relationship to the integration of pupils with special educational needs. None of this is surprising, as it is a movement which has gathered pace during the 1990s and which has its roots not in theory or research findings but in beliefs around human rights and equality of access and opportunity. Inclusion is a term that can refer to any group of pupils who have been segregated or discriminated against either in terms of access to educational opportunities or equity of provision or support once in a placement. It does not just cover children with disabilities but can also refer to ethnic or religious groups who may suffer discrimination. Exclusion of children who pose severe behaviour difficulties in schools represent a growing group and attention is beginning to focus upon such children whose educational prospects are severely impaired by exclusion. In the wider context, 'social exclusion', which indicates a large group of children and adults who are excluded from the normal 'walks of life' or 'courses of action' is a term which is now in common use in political, social and educational circles.

In 1994, UNESCO issued the Salamanca World Statement on Special Needs Education that called for the inclusion of pupils with special educational needs in mainstream schools and this has been adopted as a basis for recent educational policy documents in many countries, including the United Kingdom. Policy documents such as *Excellence in Schools* state: Where children do have special educational needs there are strong educational, social and moral grounds for their education in mainstream schools (DfEE 1997, 34).

It is clear, therefore that this movement has strong political and international backing as well as a forceful body of advocates from the disabled community and their supporters. Mainstream classroom teachers are a key group who need to be involved in the planning and delivery of inclusive education and therefore it is important that this wider context is understood.

Many teachers are puzzled by the change in terminology from integration to inclusion and there are no universally agreed definitions of either term that might clarify matters. However, Walker 1995 attempts to contrast the two approaches and Figure 1.1 shows an adaptation of Walker's model showing some of the characteristics of each approach.

Integration emphasis	Inclusion emphasis
Needs of 'special' students are different Identification of specific needs and recognition that these are different from the norm in some way	**Rights of all students** A philosophy that stresses the rights that all students have to a range of experiences etc.
Changing/remedying the subject Specific aspects of curriculum delivery might be adapted to meet special needs	**Changing the school** Whole school organisation recognises centrally the need to be flexible and continually stretching the boundaries of what is possible
Benefits to the student with special needs of being integrated Principles of normalisation and mainstream experiences acknowledged as important	**Benefits to all students of including all** Equal benefit to all pupils of having a full range of individual needs within the school
Professional, specialist expertise and formal support Singling out a pupil by virtue of their difficulties to require on-going attention from professionals and targeted support	**Informal support and the expertise of mainstream teachers** Ensuring teachers are empowered to meet a range of needs and that support is part of the day-to-day routine of the school
Technical interventions (special teaching and therapy) Implications that specific techniques are required which are different in some fundamental way for all forms of difficulty	**Good teaching for all** Acknowledgement that all teaching needs to be reflective and responsive, but that some common principles apply in most situations

Figure 1.1   Integration or inclusion

Although this figure presents some stark contrasts, it can be used as a yardstick for schools to gauge where they are in terms of their attitudes and moves towards inclusion. Alternatively, as a tool for reflection, it can help individuals to clarify their own attitudes and beliefs concerning the education of children with special needs.

> What are your views on the inclusion or segregation of children with special needs? Can you trace back where your attitudes and beliefs have come from?

Work in one local authority has sought to help schools to evaluate where they currently are in terms of inclusion and to give guidance as to how they might make more progress. It has used the notion of self-evaluation and continuous improvement and is part of a wider school improvement programme. An audit approach is used initially, completed by staff within the school. The materials, from Bonathan, Edwards and Leadbetter 1998, are included as Appendix 1.1. This is a flexible resource but is best used by staff working within the school, with an interest in special educational needs.

Psychological basis for inclusion

Psychology has been the driving force in contributing to our understanding of human motivation and this is addressed in more detail in other chapters in this book. However, it is important to understand the fundamental importance of basic needs when we consider the appropriateness of different forms of education. As long ago as 1943, Maslow described a hierarchy of basic human needs which he felt we all strive to meet, at ascending levels from the most basic to more sophisticated needs and it is this hierarchy, Maslow suggests, that governs our drives and motivation. He prioritised human needs into five levels, which are shown in Figure 1.2.

From the figure it can be seen that 'belonging' is a very basic human need occurring once physiological needs and safety needs are fulfilled. This is something we can all

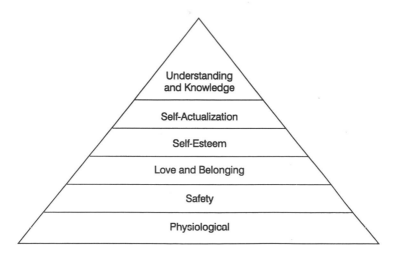

Figure 1.2   A hierarchy of needs
Based on A. H. Maslow, 'A theory of human motivation', *Psychol. Rev.*, **50**, 370–396 (1943)

recognise from experiences in childhood and often in later life. The need to feel part of a group, not 'different' in some way is important for all of us. Therefore, segregation or separation from peers can have a profound effect on children. Continuing this argument, for all children to belong to their neighbourhood communities and schools they need to be included from the start. For most pre-school children this can occur but often decisions are made at school age which set the path for a child's educational future.

Inclusion, as Micheline Mason, a disability rights spokesperson, points out, is not something that can be done to us. It is something we have to participate in for it to be real (Pugh and Macrae 1995). This word **participation** is important as it implies activity, rather than passivity and meaningful experiences rather than token placements, either at a locational, social or functional level.

Although it is acknowledged that for inclusion to work well there needs to be support at all levels from the Local Education Authority through to whole-school policy level and including the parent and pupil, in many cases, it is the class teacher who is the prime mover in designing the learning environment and learning programmes for a range of children with a huge variety of needs within the classroom. This chapter will therefore move on to address some of these difficulties and consider approaches that have been found to be successful in promoting inclusion.

Taking account of the individual

The National Curriculum provides a framework for teachers to plan and deliver the curriculum across each school year but it does far more than this. It provides yardsticks against which children's attainments can be measured and alongside this, means by which their rates of progress can be monitored. We are therefore all working within an educational environment where information is available and indeed required of us; this can be seen as a daunting administrative task or as an essential tool for planning our teaching and delivery – more likely for most teachers it is a bit of both!

Using a simple cyclical model, various phases can be implemented in order to provide effective teaching for the pupil. A model as shown in Figure 1.3 includes all essential elements.

GATHER DATA/ASSESS

MONITOR/EVALUATE   INTERVENE

Figure 1.3   Model for using information

Alongside National Curriculum information, which is available for all children, there will be children with special educational needs who are identified on the school's special needs register at one of the Code of Practice DfEE 1994 stages. Therefore, this means that there has been some measure of concern expressed, ranging from an early class teacher observation that the child seems to be experiencing a measure of difficulty in a particular subject area, to a child with a statement of their special educational needs who has a major disability and has individual support allocated specifically for them. For each child with special needs, more specific assessment and planning will need to be undertaken.

Chapter 2 looks at optimal learning environments for children, taking a broad perspective, and examines ways of improving the classroom environment for all children. Likewise this chapter, focusing as it does upon the individual, also has wider implications for all pupils. Good teaching practice, however and wherever it occurs is equally applicable for all children, whether or not they have special educational needs. A skilled teacher will be able to run a successful classroom using generally applicable routines, methods and techniques *but* will also be able to take account of individual needs within this setting. How then, can this be done?

Information gathering

It should be an increasingly rare event for a pupil to arrive in a class with no information about them available to the teacher. National Curriculum and SEN records should be transferred with the pupil in order that programmes can recommence at the point where they were left. However, inevitably, there may be some chasing of information, particularly from services or agencies who have been involved with children and families and who may not know that the children have moved. Therefore, either via the Special Needs Coordinator (SENCO) or the head teacher, it is vital that the class teacher, obtains all available information.

This is not the only source of information that a teacher can access. Where appropriate and possible, taking some time to talk to the pupil in depth can reveal not only their interests and some background information, but information about their linguistic skills, their previous schooling, programmes and levels of support. We will turn to involving pupils in their own learning later in Chapter 5, but using them as an information source is often neglected.

Alongside this, both formal and informal contact with families is vital in terms of obtaining information about such matters as:

- what has worked well in the past and what has not met with success both at home and at school;
- the family's hopes for the placement;
- the level of support which is likely to be available within the home.

Remember that this can take place at the information gathering stage. By treating parental information in a serious and professional manner you are more likely to enlist the parents' support at the intervention stage.

Assimilating and analysing the information

Often when we are confronted by a new problem situation, even though there are resources and information available (a new pupil might arrive with a bulging file and support on hand) it sometimes seems impossible to know where to begin to work with the pupil. Some time spent analysing the wealth of information and different viewpoints, using some of the suggestions outlined above, is time well spent. If the class teacher is able to do this in a collaborative manner with a supportive and informed colleague e.g. the SENCO, so much the better.

By using a simple listing technique to identify all the apparent difficulties and then using a hypothesis-testing approach, considering all the possible reasons or causes for a particular concern, a way forward can usually be found. Miller (1991, p. 197) gives an example of a boy of eight whose behaviour in class is described as disruptive and restless. He offers 13 different hypotheses or possibilities to account for the boy's behaviour; some at a physiological or neurological level, others from a developmental or cognitive point of view and yet others from a social angle. Any of these possible explanations could have been used as the basis of a plan of action.

When there are a number of competing concerns, it can be difficult to decide which one to work on. A problem solving approach, see Leadbetter and Leadbetter (1993, p. 74), offers a way forward and within this, asking a series of questions in order to select a priority can be a useful technique. Questions such as:

- How serious is the problem?
- Is it a problem for other people?
- How many children are involved?
- How much time is taken up?
- How often does the problem happen?
- Is the pupil likely to want to work on the problem?

Variations on these themes, adapted to fit with the particular situation within the school and classroom can then lead on to more formalised planning and negotiation both in terms of the content and the process of the teaching.

> Think of a pupil presenting difficulties for you at the moment or at a previous time. Try using one of the above approaches to analyse the situation and anticipate some outcomes. Which approach felt most useful or were you able to utilise elements of both approaches?

Planning and negotiating

Children with special needs will derive the support they need from a number of sources and it is important, when plans are being made, that all opportunities are considered. In some cases class teachers do not have access to any extra help, but this is increasingly rare as the funding for children with additional needs is gradually being transferred directly to schools. Therefore, children who are deemed to be at the early stages of the Code of Practice DfEE 1994 should have an allocation of time on a regular basis which is used to address their specific targets. This time could be spent with the teacher, a learning assistant, the SENCO or even an older pupil or parent who is working within a planned programme and who has received appropriate training.

The 'how, where and when' this time is used, should be the main discussion item of all those involved with the pupil and this often takes place at the IEP (Individual Education Plan) review meeting. Implementation of the National Literacy Strategy

1998, with its recommended structure for the literacy hour to be carried out in all primary classrooms will need to take into account special needs pupils. A key question will be whether the support should be within the class or outside of the class. Such a simple issue is in fact more complicated than might appear at first as the timing, the nature of the task, the curriculum areas which will be missed if the child is not present and the relationship between the support worker and the child are all factors which can influence the success of the support.

In some schools decisions of this nature may be taken out of the individual teacher's hands if there is a policy of no individual withdrawal within the school. In such a case, it is important for the teacher to be clear about the focus of support and then to exert influence over how and when it is used. For instance, if it is agreed that a pupil is entitled to an hour a day of individual support, provided as additional support by the LEA via a statement of the child's special needs, and additional to this the child receives 30 minutes a day of support from within the school's own resources, as part of a small group, the class teacher needs to take the role of manager and planner of this time, in conjunction with the SENCO for the school. Within the busy school day with all the multitude of demands on the class teacher, it can be very easy for this time to be squandered if the support is not targeted and integrated into the class life.

Implementing and reviewing a plan

Once a plan has been agreed and the support mechanisms are in place, the implementation process begins. Most Individual Education Plans (IEPs) will have a review date set and this end point is important, as it will provide a summative (final, cumulative) review of the success of the programme and the progress made by the child. However, this date might be half a term or a term away and so it is important that formative (ongoing, informative, detailed) assessments occur along the way to ensure that the targets were set appropriately and that the help is being deployed efficiently. One way of ensuring that this happens is to employ an assessment-through-teaching approach, where the regular teaching is always informed by a brief curriculum-related or criterion-referenced assessment. Solity and Raybould 1988 describe this approach in detail where they devote a whole chapter to explaining the process of assessment through teaching. However, essentially it involves regular mini-tests of the current skill levels of a child *in the particular area that is being targeted at the time.* Typical examples might be when a child is learning phonic skills, number bonds or sight words This sensitive, regular micro-level testing can inform the teaching process and also provide extremely detailed and useful records on which to base future work.

A second useful approach that ensures that the support and teaching time available is used optimally is to consider the work of one of the great cognitive psychologists, Vygotsky (see Daniels 1996). It is impossible to describe his ideas in any depth in a book such as this but his contribution to our understanding of children's learning has been substantial. He describes the process of learning as always being in relation to a social context and he emphasises the dynamic role of the teacher as someone who provides help at an appropriate level for the child, neither too little help which leaves the child floundering and making unhelpful mistakes, nor too much help which may preclude the development of understanding and cognitive processing on the part of the child. This balance requires a great deal of sensitivity and skill on the part of the teacher. Wood *et al*. 1976 used the term 'scaffolding' to describe the levels and types of help which can be employed, dependent upon the child's learning style, the social context and the current task.

For teaching to be effective it is vital that the teacher becomes conscious of the various important factors which impinge on the learning process, not least of which is the child's own preferred learning style. Vygotsky used the term 'Zone of Proximal Development' or ZPD as it is sometimes known, to describe the area of learning which the child and teacher are moving into together and this can be a useful concept to keep in mind when planning the implementation of a programme. A crucial factor in successful scaffolding is that the teacher should **mediate** the pupil's progress through their zone of proximal development. Additionally, the use of peers as resources should not be underestimated when considering potential methods to scaffold a pupil's learning.

An example of a teacher being aware of a child's ZPD might be during a child's acquisition of the skill of double-digit addition. The child might be taught the basic building block skills necessary but then be left to explore the relationships and patterns of the numbers in order that they begin to understand the logic and rules of the computation. A good teacher would be checking that the manipulations and explorations were positive and enjoyable for the child, indicating that the child was moving towards an understanding of the concept. If, however, the child's responses were rather meaningless and floundering, this would indicate that the child was likely to be working beyond their ZPD and would need more 'scaffolding', perhaps in the way of more instruction or exemplification.

Consider a task you are currently trying to teach to a particular pupil. Can you think of ways in which you might be able to 'scaffold' the child's learning to ensure success? Note down any techniques, additional to those already tried, that might be applicable.

Techniques for supporting inclusion

At the start of this chapter we talked about inclusion being more of a process than a state. Therefore it is important to consider the social context within a class both for children with special needs and also for the benefit of all the children. Many classes nowadays acknowledge the importance of group work and the widespread use of 'Circle Time' in many primary schools is a testament to this (see Chapter 3 for information on this technique). However, conducting group work is not easy and it is rare for teachers to have received any specific training in this area. Lack of specific training is one of the main reasons that teachers shy away from group work especially when the group includes pupils with special needs. It is perhaps helpful to consider two separate strands; the **skills** needed and the **structures** to make it work. Some of the skills which teachers need and in turn which need to be developed by the children are commonly found in use in counselling psychology. The following skills are important when working with groups:

- listening carefully and attentively to what is said;
- asking questions in a facilitative and non-judgemental manner;
- giving positive feedback whenever possible;
- paraphrasing what a child has said to ensure their intended meaning is conveyed;
- linking and including statements from different group members;
- being able to disclose your own feelings.

In terms of structures and techniques that can facilitate group work, there are now many published works that provide useful materials. Techniques include: circle work, pair work, using different roles within groups, problem solving groups and many others. (See Chapter 3.)

There are also techniques that have been developed more specifically with children with specific needs in mind, whether these are learning-related, related to emotional or behavioural needs or to more specific special educational needs. One such technique is called 'Circle of friends' and this was developed in Ontario, Canada where inclusion has been underway for many years. The technique, alongside many others, is described in detail in Stainback and Stainback 1996, but essentially involves a process of focusing on a particular child's need for support and utilising the peers in the class to provide this in a structured but voluntary way. It has been successful with a wide range of children and in particular with children with autism and behaviour difficulties.

> Are there any other techniques that you use in class or with groups of children that are designed to improve the quality of the social relations in the class? Could these be shared with other staff in the school as a tool to aid the move towards inclusion?

What is different about inclusive approaches?

The theme of this chapter has been that there is nothing essentially different about the teaching and approaches for many (but not all) pupils with special needs that would not be considered good teaching practice for all children. So in one sense, the answer to the question posed in this section is *nothing*. However, from another perspective, what is different is *everything*, when consideration of attitudes and values is taken into account, and it is this factor which will be crucial in promoting successful inclusion. The attitudes become quickly reflected in systems and approaches and some of these differences are summarised clearly by Porter 1995 who compares traditional and inclusionary approaches, (see Figure 1.4).

These factors indicate that we have a long way to go to make classrooms more inclusive, but this will be of necessity a step-by-step approach.

Thomas *et al.* 1998, p. 14 highlight a key notion which is fundamental to inclusion: 'A central aspect of an inclusion project must therefore lie in the deconstruction of the idea that only special people are equipped and qualified to teach special children.'

This statement can be both frightening and empowering to the new teacher faced with a class of children with diverse needs. However, with support and guidance of a collaborative nature, gratifying results can and will be achieved.

Traditional approach (which may include integration)	Inclusionary approach
Focus on student	Focus on classroom
Assessment of study by specialist	Examine teaching/learning factors
Diagnostic prescriptive outcomes	Collaborative problem-solving
Student programme	Strategies for teachers
Placement in appropriate programme	Adaptive and support regular classroom environment

Figure 1.4   Traditional vs inclusionary approaches

Further reading

Gross, J. (1996) *Special Educational Needs in the Primary School. A practical guide.* Buckingham: Open University Press.

Lindsay, G. and Miller, A. (eds) (1991) *Psychological Services for Primary Schools.* Essex: Longman.

Mills, J. and Mills, R. W. (1995) *Primary School People. Getting to know your colleagues.* London: Routledge.

Thomas, G., Walker, D. and Webb, J. (1998) *The Making of the Inclusive School.* London: Routledge.

Tilstone, C., Florian, L. and Rose, R. (eds) (1998) *Promoting Inclusive Practice.* London: Routledge.

CHAPTER 2

Understanding the learning environment

Gren Knight

Introduction

What do we mean by the learning environment? It is a term that has been used, often quite loosely, to refer to several aspects of the educational process. Providing a rich and stimulating environment in which children learn through exploration and discovery has been one influential notion for example. The term has also been used to describe the nature and content of the curriculum. This chapter takes two distinct and more focused perspectives. First it introduces what psychological theory and research has to contribute to the physical environment in which learning takes place. Secondly it discusses the psychosocial environment that exists in the minds of children and teachers as they work together. Each of these perspectives is informed by extensive research but application of this to classroom practice is, in general, fairly recent. The purpose of this chapter is to encourage an active consideration of the implications of the physical and psychosocial learning environments for children's progress and for the emotional and physical wellbeing of both children and teachers.

Ergonomics: A brief historical perspective

The area of psychology that is concerned with the interaction between people and the physical environment is called ergonomics. Another term, used more often in the USA, is 'Human Factors', derived from the focus on the human factor in person–machine interactions. An important early influence was F. W. Taylor's time and motion studies around the start of the 20th century. Taylor was an engineer who recognised the inefficiency of many of the industrial practices he witnessed and set out to demonstrate how managers and workers could benefit from a more scientific approach. This required a detailed analysis of what was involved in a job, deciding on the most efficient way of doing it and designing the layout of the workplace and the tools involved to support this. Employees were then trained in the one best approach and rewarded for above average performance.

There are several interesting parallels with the educational process. However, the principles that Taylor identified are still a major influence on workplace practice today. Although anyone applying them can be criticised for taking too simple a view of what motivates people (e.g. the value of variety in a job and the importance of personal satisfaction for sustained motivation), the main point to remember is that Taylor drew attention to the value of thinking about adapting tools and the environment to improve productivity rather than simply requiring people to fit in with the environment it was convenient to present them with.

Thinking about design

There are countless examples in everyday life of devices or processes that have irritating features that just do not fit in with the way we want to use them. Despite a much greater value being put on good design these days often it is financial or aesthetic considerations that have more influence than a careful assessment of how people use the item or environment in question. Some examples found in schools that illustrate this include chair and table design, the acoustic consequences of classroom design and furnishing, corridor and door design and the layout of classroom furniture. However there are many more.

Bad designs which have annoyed me:

List examples of items or layouts that have caused frustration or have even been dangerous. You could involve pupils in this: 1 point for a non-educational design, 2 points for something in school!

The most important principle in 'Human Factors' is that of user-centred design. People are very adaptable but something that is designed to fit the natural or best way for users will promote efficient use, better outcomes and reduce errors and difficulties. Environments should be designed to fit people rather than people having to be trained to adapt to environments designed to other criteria.

Psychology and common sense

Does this, you might ask, involve an application of psychological theory? Couldn't a lot of these problems be solved with common sense? This is an important question to answer as it is based on a misunderstanding of what psychology can offer and an overestimation of the power of common sense. Howarth 1987 provides a neat discussion of this. He gives an illustration of the illusion of understanding created by common sense in the contrasting proverbs e.g. 'too many cooks spoil the broth', but 'many hands make light work'! While common sense provides reasonably reliable responses to common situations it is not so good at analysing uncommon or new events. The wisdom acquired by experience gives intuitive guides to action rather than analytic concepts with which to describe and think about the nature of complex tasks, particularly tasks which are posing problems. This leads to a tendency to describe a problem in terms of what the solution might be – children are noisy and unruly in corridors (forget the acoustics and design of corridors, just keep the children quiet); children are not sitting properly in their chairs (chairs may not be comfortable but children can still be expected to sit still and stay in their places). Solutions like this beg the question. Ideas about effective solutions should come after the problem has been thoroughly investigated, with attention to all the elements involved (the environment as well as people), and not before.

> Think of one or two common sense solutions to problems in school. Consider alternatives to the obvious solution by analysing the problem with a focus on altering the environment rather than the people involved.

Human error

One of the most frequent common sense explanations for problems in people–environment interactions is human error. This is often cited as the cause in catastrophic incidents like plane crashes. Less obviously it is also a very common response to many problems in school in the sense that children and teachers are expected to adapt to circumstances that actually encourage problems to arise. In the absence of malicious intent (although even this can be encouraged by bad design sometimes), five factors can underlie the emergence of problems.

1. The way in which something is designed to be used. For example a computer keyboard, a handle for opening a door or a system like registration or detentions.
2. Training: How to work in a workshop, how to use a computer, how to use the library etc.
3. Physical stress: For example physical discomfort caused by inappropriate chair design.
4. Psychological stress: For example difficulty with lesson content, distracting noise, unwelcome interactions with others.
5. Past experience: 'In my last school we did it this way'.

Analysing difficulties in schooling using these five points as alternative perspectives will produce a more sophisticated understanding leading to more successful ways forward. Doing this by actively involving the people concerned is particularly important.

Listen to the children

The second 'Human Factors' principle to bear in mind is the importance of consulting the user when designing or analysing a problem that involves people interacting with things or with the environment. Oates and Evans 1990 report an example of school-based research in ergonomics that is a comparatively rare published illustration of what may be possible in school. They involved a class of Year 7 Science students in an investigation of how well classroom furniture fitted the users. Chairs were measured and users surveyed to collect demographic (age) and anthropometric (stature, upper leg length, popliteal height*, and shoulder height above seat) data, together with

---

* Popliteal height is an important anthropometic measurement in chair design. It is the distance from floor to the mid part of the back of the knee when someone is standing up straight.

reports of discomfort and information about problems in use. The results showed that 87 per cent of subjects reported that their chairs were uncomfortable some or all of the time. Only 22 per cent reported no discomfort. Mid to low back pain was cited by 66 per cent of respondents. 81 per cent considered that at least one school activity (reading, writing, concentration, other) was restricted by the seating used.

Are they sitting comfortably?

Oates and Evans report a good example of how pupils can be involved in studying their learning environment. Their focus on school furniture also introduces a topic which raises a variety of issues illustrating the importance of an ergonomic perspective on the learning environment. Dr Aage Chresten Mandal, a Danish Orthopaedics Specialist, makes a persuasive criticism of conventional chair design in his book *The Seated Man: Homo Sedens* 1985. He suggests that until 200 years ago most people sat on benches or on the floor and that historically chairs have been symbols of dignity used to emphasise or raise social status (consider this with respect to chairs in school!) He argues that the cultural value of sitting upright on chairs (in order to emphasise social status) was further encouraged when, as office work increased with industrialisation, factors like Victorian moral values and the design of women's clothing also emphasised upright postures. Mandal attributes the design of the traditional school desk to a German designer called Staffel. This included upright seating and a sloping work surface that were quite high by modern standards.

However, from an orthopaedic perspective Mandal argues that the need for an upright posture has never been justified, even though it continues to influence modern school furniture design. In the 1940s separate chairs and tables began to replace combined desks and seats. These allowed more flexible arrangements (e.g. grouping tables) and stacking. The furniture was also generally lower than earlier designs. Mandal's view is that 'all our present experience suggests that the changes resulted in a catastrophic deterioration in the way children sit at their work' (Mandal 1985). He suggests a radically different type of seating that is based on orthopaedic analysis and aims for minimal levels of stress on the back while supporting the two main activities children are engaged in at school: listening/looking and writing/reading. His design is for a higher chair with a seat contoured to support forward sitting for working as well as sitting back to listen, and a raised table with a sloping surface and footrest. (See Figure 2.1.)

Mandal type chair design

The ergonomic arguments for this design are persuasive (although not without criticism) and have been introduced as an alternative European standard to that which describes traditional school chairs and tables. Bearing in mind the reports of back pain and discomfort arising from conventional seating and evidence (e.g. Knight and Noyes 1998) that seating design affects on-task behaviour, investment in well designed school furniture should be a priority.

Undoubtedly, the notion that people should adapt to the environment still prevails and applies particularly to children. (Teachers often have somewhat better

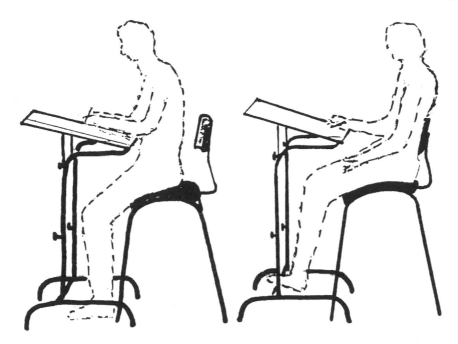

Figure 2.1   Mandal's chair design

quality furniture.) Cost is also a major factor and one that in recent years has probably been an overriding consideration. However, there is a good deal that can be done at little cost. Children often sit on seats and work at tables which are too high or too low (e.g. Knight 1994.) Manufacturers offer guidance on this for teachers and periodic checks should be undertaken. Simply alerting pupils to the issues is helpful as is training for both teachers and pupils. The National Back Pain Association provide useful advice in a paper entitled 'Furniture plus Fitness = Healthy Attentive Pupils' (Taylor 1997). This is a brief guide to school furniture and includes an outline of recent developments and research and the features to look out for in good product design.

Assessing the physical environment

When assessing the physical environment, there is no substitute for taking an ergonomic perspective informed by the considerations described above. Reducing the amount of 'adapting to the environment' that is required in school will improve staff and pupil performance and involving the users as to how to do this is very important.

Assessments can be done informally, simply through incidental observation and discussion with staff and pupils. However this is not far removed from a common sense approach, the pitfalls of which were discussed earlier. The Classroom Ergonomics Checklist (CEC), Knight 1999, offers a more systematic approach which at the same time is flexible enough to be used in a variety of classrooms. (See Appendix 2.1.)

Fundamental to effective use of the checklist is accurate identification of the main activities for which the room is used. Many judgements of ergonomic suitability will depend upon this. For example we know that pupils are on-task more of the time when working individually if their seating is arranged in rows rather than grouped round tables. On the other hand if discussion activity or group work is required there are implications for a different arrangement of chairs and tables (Wheldall 1982).

In practice, classrooms must support a variety of activities and they may be less suitable for some than for others. If ergonomic suitability is a significant problem consideration should be given to making changes perhaps to the activity or to use of a more suitable room.

The second important point to bear in mind in assessing the environment is the principle of consulting the user. The CEC can be completed by an observer alone but a much more valid assessment is likely if staff and pupils are consulted. Indeed the checklist is well suited to completion by a teacher in discussion with pupils, or by a teacher in the light of individual pupil comment. This is important as pupil feedback is likely to vary depending on their usual seating position (e.g. sitting by a radiator or near the door).

The CEC identifies sixteen major categories which can be given an overall rating on a three point scale. Each category has several prompts that probably need to be considered in most classrooms. The person completing the checklist should make the overall judgement after considering each of the prompts and making notes about any concerns arising from them, or other features of the room relevant to the category being considered. The main activities for which the room is used should always be borne in mind when completing the CEC and, as emphasised above, judgements based on the views of the users will be more valid than those of an independent observer acting alone.

The Summary section of the CEC allows an overall score to be calculated simply by adding the ratings for each feature. If this is done it needs to be borne in mind that the score is not based on a weighted rating. A room may be ergonomically very unsuitable for its purpose if only one or two features are particularly problematic. However it will still obtain a comparatively high score.

For this reason it is preferable to use the final section of the CEC to list the features that cause concern and identify possible solutions, many of which may be quite simple and cost free to implement. Once again involving the people who use the room, both teachers and pupils, in finding solutions is the best approach.

Complete the CEC for your classroom. Then involve the pupils in an assessment. Did you have different perspectives? Jointly plan some solutions to any problems identified.

The psychosocial environment

Undoubtedly the term 'psychosocial environment' sounds rather like psychological jargon. However it does clearly identify as something tangible the way in which children and teachers perceive the general nature of interactions between people and the values, assumptions and preferences that influence these interactions. Terms like ethos, climate, atmosphere, culture, tone, or ambience have a less precise feel to them.

The fact that so many different terms are in use for much the same thing probably reflects both the importance of the general idea and the lack of precision about what exactly people are referring to! The situation is not helped by the same terms being used to refer to slightly different things in the extensive research literature on issues like organisational climate, learning styles, school culture, ethos and so on. In the hope of clarifying matters a little, if only for this chapter, the following definitions may be helpful.

Organisational Climate refers to the consensus of people's perceptions about how a particular organisation (e.g. school) or part of an organisation (e.g. class or group) deals with its members and its external environment (e.g. other people). (Szilagyi 1983).

Some definitions of **Organisational Culture** provide a slightly different slant. It can be simply thought of as 'taken for granted' and 'shared meanings' that people assign to their social surroundings. This is broadly consistent with Schein 1990 who describes culture in terms of superficial behaviours and habits of interaction (*artefacts*), the underlying *values* held by members of an organisation that influence the way they behave and deeper, sometimes unrecognised, basic *assumptions* that have a more general profound effect.

Try to identify some of the 'artefacts' that may reveal something about your school's organisational culture. Think of the way people interact, physical features of the school, routine ways of doing things. What underlying values do these suggest?

Examples: – Parents wait outside school to collect pupils vs. parents enter the building.
– Location of head teacher's office in relation to the rest of the school.

To make sense of the terms it may be helpful to think of the **Psychosocial Learning Environment** in similar terms to Szilagyi's definition of organisational climate, as referring to the perceptions of teachers and pupils about their shared situation and relationships. Culture may be seen to include this but to refer also to the underlying values and assumptions which affect individual perceptions and which may be inconsistent with how people actually behave some of the time.

The importance of the learning environment

Various observations have been made about the psychosocial learning environment and school effectiveness. Mortimore *et al.* 1988, for example, found atmosphere more pleasant in effective schools and linked this with less emphasis on punishment and critical control, more emphasis on praise and reward, the active promotion of self-control and, amongst other factors, time devoted to non-school conversations between teachers and pupils reflecting an interest in pupils as individuals. Research has consistently linked factors like these with pupil progress and positive behaviour. Stephenson and Smith 1987, for example, found that lower incidences of bullying were positively associated with the frequency with which staff articulated positive views towards pupils and emphasised the importance of positive supportive relationships.

There is a general acceptance that climate affects what goes on in a school and that both climate and culture are psychological entities that are quite hard to alter. OFSTED inspections require comment in terms of 'Behaviour and Discipline' and 'Spiritual and Moral Development'. The former is judged by the extent to which the attitudes and actions of pupils contribute to or restrict effective learning in class and the quality of life and functioning of the school as an orderly community. The Spiritual and Moral development of pupils is judged in terms of their contributions and responses to the ethos of the school i.e. the principles for which it stands and the values and attitudes it fosters.

A good deal of work has been undertaken in the USA and in Australia on the psychosocial classroom environment and its effect on performance and behaviour. As in ergonomics the key idea that has developed is the need for person-environment fit. Fraser (1986) suggests for example that the degree of fit between individual and environment affects performance, stress and satisfaction – and thus in turn the behaviour of both pupils and teachers. Based on an analysis of a variety of studies involving altogether over 17,000 children he reported better achievement in classes which children perceived as having greater cohesiveness, satisfaction, goal direction and low levels of disorganisation and friction.

Assessing the learning environment

These ideas are all very well but they remain somewhat intangible in practice without means of assessing perceptions of the psychosocial environment. Fraser 1986 and others have developed a variety of simple questionnaires that can be used with both primary and secondary pupils and with teachers to provide information about individual and group perceptions of the psychosocial environment. Some of these questionnaires also touch on the physical environment in so far as it is seen as contributing to other psychological constructs about the group.

Two of the questionnaires that have been used in this country are the My Class Inventory (MCI) for 8–12 year olds and the associated and more detailed Learning Environment Inventory (LEI) for pupils aged 12–19.

The Learning Environment Inventory (LEI), Fraser *et al*. 1982, has 105 statements that relate to 15 dimensions of classroom climate. Respondents express their degree of agreement or disagreement with each statement on a four point scale. The questionnaire is easy to complete and to score and is reasonably reliable. A list of the 15 dimensions of climate or environment that are covered by the LEI gives a flavour of its content area. They are:

Cohesiveness	Friction	Democracy
Diversity	Goal direction	Cliqueness
Formality	Favouritism	Satisfaction
Speed	Difficulty	Disorganisation
Material environment	Apathy	Competitiveness

The My Class Inventory (MCI) is a simplified form of the LEI and can be used with younger pupils and older students who have reading difficulties. It contains just five of the LEI's dimensions, (Cohesiveness, Friction, Satisfaction, Difficulty and Competitiveness), has simplified wording and requires only a Yes/No response. There are 25 items altogether.

> Predict how your class would rate each of the broad categories of the MCI. Then discuss this with some of the pupils. Is there a consensus? Any surprises? What could you do to improve any problem areas?

Questionnaires like these can be used in various ways with both individuals and whole classes. Bearing in mind the research on the importance of person–environment fit it is particularly useful to ask children to complete the questionnaire twice. First of all on the basis of how things actually are and then to describe their preferred environment. Discrepancies between the two can then be addressed. Similarly, individual responses that differ notably from the overall consensus are informative in assisting individual pupils. Discussing their perceptions in more detail or differentiating aspects of the environment to suit their preferences are options. The questionnaires can be used to reassess perceptions after a period during which a teacher has tried to influence a change. Two studies which have reported on the use of learning environment questionnaires in this country are by Wright, Gallagher and Lombardi 1991, and Burden and Fraser 1994.

Wright, Gallagher and Lombardi 1991 used the My Class Inventory with 246 primary school children from ten classes in seven schools. Children were allowed as much time as they wished to complete the questionnaire and were helped with reading when necessary. In most cases the questionnaire was administered by an Eucational Psychologist but in the tenth class it was the teacher. Wright *et al.* suggest that the presence of the teacher may have influenced the judgements of the children though they do not expand on this. Certainly the questionnaire does not require special training and is open for use by teachers.

In Australia, Fisher and Fraser 1981 established norms based on the scores provided by 2305 children who completed the My Class Inventory. Wright *et al*'s study which was based on a smaller group (246) showed some differences from the Australian norms. The British children thought that their classrooms were less cohesive but experienced less friction than the Australian pupils. They were significantly more satisfied with their classrooms but indicated a higher level of difficulty with the work. These differences need to be borne in mind if the Australian norms are used when interpreting the MCI scores. Wright *et al.* report on the value of producing histograms illustrating pupil responses to statements on each scale as a stimulus to discussion, and this may be a more useful approach.

Burden and Fraser 1994 discuss the use of several classroom environment questionnaires as a means of assessing the ethos or climate of a school. They consider the use of a questionnaire called the School Level Environment Questionnaire (SLEQ) to assess teacher's perceptions of their actual school environments and how they would prefer those environments to be. Typical use of the questionnaires is with a whole staff group completing both forms, discussing the results and their implications, making changes and re-evaluating in due course.

Burden and Fraser suggest that questionnaires like the SLEQ could be used in conjunction with questionnaires that elicit pupil perceptions, or simply by itself, relating results to outcomes like teacher job satisfaction or pupil achievement and morale. There are many possibilities.

The My Class Inventory and the Learning Environment Inventory are to be found in Fraser 1986. The School Level Environment Questionnaire (SLEQ) is part of the article by Burden and Fraser (1994).

Conclusion

This chapter describes two perspectives on the learning environment that a teacher should find fairly easy to apply in their own classrooms. Although both have significant implications for pupil progress they offer approaches that have not been widely used. Hopefully the discussion will whet the appetite and, as well as providing some practical ideas in itself, will stimulate further reading and investigation. Certainly there is a need for a lot more publication of small-scale studies in both of the approaches to the learning environment described in this chapter.

Further reading

Fraser, B. J. (1986) *Classroom Environment*. London: Croom Helm.

Knight, G. and Noyes, J. (1999) 'Children's behaviour and the design of school furniture', *Ergonomics*, **42** pp. 747–60.

Mandal, A. C. (1985) *The Seated Man: Homo Sedens* (3rd edn), Klampenborg, Denmark: Dafnia Publications.

Taylor, J. (1997) *Furniture Plus Fitness = Healthy Attentive Pupils*. The National Back Pain Association.

CHAPTER 3

Managing the social dynamics of the classroom

Sue Morris

Introduction

For many teachers, the challenge of meeting children's diverse individual needs in the classroom setting can be a daunting one. Class size can be seen as a limiting factor. There will be some pupils in the class who clearly need a high level of individual instruction if they are to progress and other pupils whose behaviour claims a high proportion of the teacher's time and attention. Some children can work quietly and constructively with little direct teacher support while others seem unable to get along together without frequent fall-outs!

One legacy of the Plowden Report, DES 1967, has been a pressure on teachers to individualise their teaching in order to maximise its relevance to individual pupils. While the value of individualised instruction is recognised, this chapter argues that the education of children in group settings is, if well managed, a great asset, rather than simply a logistic necessity or, at worst, a pedagogic nightmare.

The practice of teaching children in mixed ability classes is invaluable in:

- providing a context in which to support children's development of important social and interpersonal skills, alongside their acquisition of academic competence; and
- increasing the pool of expertise and instructional support available to each child. Children are an extremely potent resource for learning: to view them as net consumers rather than also as providers of relevant skills is to squander a rich seam of available tutorial support. Learning is fundamentally a social process.

The remainder of this chapter describes practical steps derived from social and organisational psychology that can be taken to help translate this rather idealised vision of students as a resource for one another's learning and social development into a reality. Three different, but complementary approaches will be considered:

- using knowledge of the life-cycle of social groups to craft the class into a task-oriented, mutually supportive working group;

- the establishment and use of 'Circle Time' to create a positive classroom ethos, to build students' communication skills, and to develop their competence to take responsibility for solving interpersonal problems in a democratic way;
- the ways in which different approaches to group work can be incorporated into 'routine' classroom teaching in order to enhance the quality of student learning and the self-esteem and social competence of children in the class.

Crafting the group

A classroom is an ad hoc collection of individuals: all they are guaranteed to have in common on their arrival in school is their age-range, the part of the country in which they live, and the fact that their parents have sent them to the same school. Their differences, in terms of their background experience, interests, levels of maturity, learning styles, abilities, attainments, motivation, and much more, will be likely to outweigh their similarities by a wide margin.

Individuals in the class may have little sense of group identity; it will often be the case, for instance, that girls and boys have little to do with one another, beyond exchanging insults and/or performing tricks in order to impress or provoke one another. If left unchecked, this gender segregation will have a number of negative consequences, reinforcing gender stereotyping, which will, over time, contribute to the growing under-achievement of boys in comparison with girls. Girls' greater interest in talking and reading is held to contribute to their greater skills in oracy and literacy which, in turn, as important tools for learning, contribute to academic achievement. Boys' beliefs that to be 'cool' and enjoy high status with their male peers, one must not be a 'boffin' or 'a girl', frequently militate against their conformity in the classroom or their conspicuous investment in the pursuit of academic excellence. If the social dynamics of the classroom are skilfully managed, so that boys and girls work effectively together, their different learning orientations will complement one another, so supporting the social and academic development of both sexes.

Apart from the boy–girl schism that is readily apparent in many classrooms, from a very early age, other potentially harmful divisions may occur: friendship groups can be so tight as to exclude and marginalise others; cliques based upon ethnic groupings can become established; or a class may, over time, differentiate such groups as the conforming workers, the easy riders, the passively disaffected, and the challenging non-conformists.

The Elton Report, DES 1989, states that:

> Co-operative behaviour makes any organisation more efficient, but in schools such behaviour is more than just useful ... Promoting responsible behaviour and self-discipline, and the values on which they are based, is an essential task for schools (p. 66 para 31)

As indicated above, however, cooperative behaviour cannot be assumed to be the norm. Rather, for many children, the reality of school life can be a struggle to survive within what feels like an obstacle course in which other children are competitors, or pose a threat. As Stanford, writing in 1990 noted, children in a class may have no sense of group identity; they may feel uncomfortable with other members of their class, and so be reluctant to contribute, fearing ridicule, humiliation and embarrassment. Moreover, when they do make the effort to work cooperatively, they may experience failure and frustration because they have never been taught the skills necessary for effective collaborative work.

Social psychologists in the 1970s identified a number of common stages through which most social groups progress. One of these models developed by Tuckman and Jensen in 1977, which applies to a wide range of social contexts, including those within which we, as adults operate, is summarised in Figure 3.1, as applied to the classroom setting.

Stage	Tuckman and Jensen's Model
1	**Forming** • Observing and 'sussing out' the setting and its requirements • Working out the rules • Making sense of other people • Building up familiarity (A time of low conflict)
2	**Storming** • Having taken the situation in, vying for position in the social hierarchy • Vying for role (leader, clown, expert, agony aunt ...) (A period of turbulence)
3	**Norming** • Establish norms, roles, etc • A classroom culture ('the way we do things around here') develops • A hierarchy of power and influence emerges
4	**Performing** • (If the previous stages have been negotiated successfully) the group is now ready and able to get on with the job of learning. • If negative norms have been established, there will be conflict over what and how group members perform. Effective performance of group tasks is unlikely.
5	**Adjourning** • If the group has normed and performed well, its ending will be stressful and cause turbulence. • The ending of an unsuccessful group will be a great relief, leading to the release of hitherto suppressed anger and anxiety. • Either way, the ending needs to be carefully managed if the expression of the contingent emotions is to be a positive experience for group members.

Figure 3.1 The stages of group development

The social chemistry of groups varies: some will effortlessly gel: however to assume that this will occur would be an act of optimistic naiveté. Tuckman and Jensen note that their five-stage model does not necessarily represent a single linear process: rather, during its life, a group may need to return to previous stages, and endeavour to re-negotiate these.

At worst, a class may spend a turbulent and unproductive year ricocheting between the storming and norming stages, failing to reach a point when pupils have found a way of co-existing equitably with one another or settling to their studies.

West 1994, writing about teamwork in the workplace, identifies two core dimensions that will determine whether or not the team is efficient, effective and productive. These are:

- task reflexivity: the extent to which the team is work-oriented;
- social reflexivity: the extent to which the team is concerned with the wellbeing of individuals, and the quality of relationships between team members.

He concludes that effective teams are high in both task reflexivity and social reflexivity, as evidenced by the 'Type A' team or group in Figure 3.2 below.

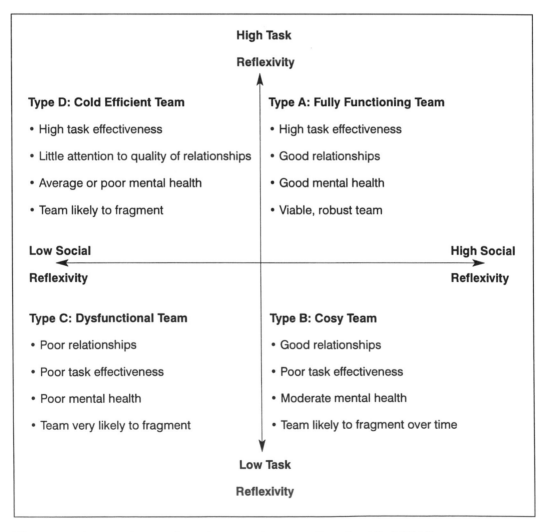

Figure 3.2   Impact of group dynamics on performance. Based on West (1994)

Translating West's ideas into classroom practice clearly suggests that we need to strive to develop both social and task reflexivity in pupils if we are to craft a fully functioning classroom group, where pupils work industriously, get along with one another, and feel secure: in other words, where the 'norming' stage of the model summarised in Figure 3.1 ensures that social and task reflexivity are instilled in the pupils, so that the class can 'perform' effectively and happily.

Before proceeding to the next section of this chapter, pause and reflect, making a note of the steps you take:

1. when you start the year with a new class, to help to establish harmonious relationships and a positive work ethos; and
2. throughout the year, to maintain and develop this climate for learning and social support, and to troubleshoot any emerging problems which threaten the 'norms' you wish to maintain.

Circle Time

The use of Circle Time can be invaluable as a forum to assist the teacher in steering the class towards the 'norms' summarised above.

Circle Time has been developed as a simple procedure which can make a strong contribution to a school's system of pastoral support, and to students' personal and social education, as well as offering many valuable opportunities for them to develop their speaking and listening skills.

The approach can also have value in creating a framework in which children's interpersonal skills can be developed, as a result of making explicit the 'social rules' necessary for effective interpersonal transactions, exposing children to models of good interpersonal and communication skills, and ensuring that feedback can be received in a sensitive and positive way. Additionally, it has value in supporting individual children, and in cementing caring interpersonal relationships within a group, and creating supportive, constructive 'norms' for mature, responsible social behaviour. Overall both the content and the process of Circle Time can have value in supporting the social development of individual children, and in contributing to the development of cohesive group dynamics.

When using Circle Time with the class, it is preferable, where possible, to seat pupils in a circle, so they can see one another, and where the physical layout confirms pupils' inclusion/involvement as members of one group.

In setting up Circle Time with a new class, it is important at the outset clearly to specify the rationale for its use, for example:

We are like a family; we will be working together and playing together for a number of years.

We will all do better, and enjoy being in this class (like our family) if we can get to know one another, respect one another, help one another, and make the effort to get on with one another.

BUT

This class has got a lot more people in it than most of our families! If we're going to be able to get to know one another so everyone who wants to can have his say, or her say, so we can talk about our problems, experiences and successes, and so we can solve some of the problems that crop up, and help people when they're having a bad time ...) we need to organise things carefully so this can happen.

It will also be necessary to introduce some 'ground-rules' to organise the procedure. Suggested ground-rules are:

- no one has to speak if she/he doesn't want to;
- only one person can speak at a time;
- try to show respect when someone is talking (this often takes courage): listen attentively, and, even if you don't agree, try to understand their point of view. No put-downs!
- everyone should be taking an active and positive part in the circle all the time, not one person talking while everyone else day-dreams!

These rules may need to be altered as time progresses, in the light of experience. During the first few Circle Time sessions detailed attention needs to be paid to the procedure, rather than the content of sessions.

The rules need to be explained and systematically reinforced (where possible by praising/commenting on their successful implementation, e.g. 'Well done! I could see you were listening attentively because you were looking at X and Y while they were talking', or 'Congratulations! I could see P, Q and R were bursting to make a point in response to what A just said, but they managed to hold on to it and wait their turn.'

Because of the focus on process, it's worth choosing some interesting or entertaining content for the first sessions, to hold pupils' attention, and to establish the expectation that Circle Time is enjoyable. Some snappy rounds where each pupil volunteers one observation on a donated theme (e.g. 'When I woke up this morning and remembered it was school today, the first thought I had was ...'), or passes, tend to prove useful in getting the Circle Time procedures moving.

It may be helpful to use a 'magic microphone' to help establish the turn-taking (rule two as above), and the idea of choosing to speak or to 'pass' (first rule above).

In the first sessions, the teacher should select the topic(s) or theme(s), and should join the circle, modelling appropriate behaviour (salient comment, attentive listening, etc.) as well as offering appropriate procedural prompts and feedback. Once the Circle procedure is established, and a climate of trust and security created, more personal and/or challenging topics and themes can form the focus for the Circle. Circle Time discussion should ideally be integrated with other group activities, to ensure that issues that arise can be processed appropriately and that the approach does not degenerate into a sterile routine.

Curry and Bromfield (1995) suggest a staged model for the use of Circle Time:

Stage 1: *Affirmation*, through use of activities in which pupils give one another positive feedback. Children can, in different pairings or groupings, be given opportunities to find out things about one another, and share these with other members of the class in a positive way, with the 'golden rules' enforced to ensure security from 'put-downs'. The Affirmation activities give opportunities to build the children's self-esteem and confidence, and to facilitate contact between them, and heighten their awareness of one another's interests, opinions, hopes, worries, and so on.

Stage 2: *Communication*, which builds on the affirming culture established through Stage 1, and further encourages the children to talk about their needs, feelings and ideas, and to listen attentively and respectfully to one another.

Stage 3: *Cooperation*. In this stage, pairing and small group activities are introduced to support the children's development of skills in working together, and making choices and decisions without causing irritation to one another.

Stage 4: *Problem-Solving*. Once affirming, collaborative norms have been established, the Circle can be used as an effective medium within which the class can address and seek solutions to emerging problems in the lives of individual children, or of the class as a whole.

Well managed and carefully structured use of Circle activities can have immense value in establishing a classroom culture within which high social and task reflexivity are the norm, where the social and academic performance of the students reaches a high standard, and where problems can be promptly addressed and resolved as they occur.

Circle Time is now in common use in primary schools in the UK. This poses problems for teachers in keeping the process fresh and interesting.

- Consider the needs of your own class. What is their previous experience of Circle Time? How could you check out their attitudes towards Circle Time, and identify the things they find most helpful and most off-putting about Circle activities, and their suggestions for making the process work even better?

Group work

The National Association for Pastoral Care in Education 1993 has published very convincing evidence for the value of group work in promoting improved academic learning outcomes for students, and in supporting their social development, self-esteem and personal wellbeing. Bennett 1995 offers an informative review of the potential benefits of group work, to which he clearly has a strong commitment. However, he sounds a note of caution, emphasising that group work must be skilfully managed if its rich potential is to be realised.

Amongst the points which he raises are that:

- children will not automatically be able to work together: we need to teach them the prerequisite social and organisational skills;
- teachers need to give thoughtful consideration to the nature of the learning they aim to facilitate, and select the approach to group work that will be most appropriate (e.g. collaborative group work, where the children work together on a shared task, cf. use of jigsaw groups, where children each select one element of the group task to pursue independently, so that the overall group response comprises the 'piecing together' of group members' individual work to form an integrated whole); and
- the size and composition of groups is a key determinant of their success. Bennett recommends four as an ideal size; he argues that both single sex and mixed groups

can work well, but notes that where boys outnumber girls in a group, this is likely to prove problematic; he further notes that high ability students perform well in both ability-based and mixed ability groups, whereas low attaining pupils are likely to get very little out of working in ability-based groups, but to thrive in mixed ability groups (provided that children have been taught how to work in groups, so that all members are included).

It is the first of the caveats summarised above that the following paragraphs will discuss further.

Thacker 1990 describes some interesting work he has undertaken with both primary and secondary-aged students, using 'routine' group work to help the children develop social and task reflexivity, and become more skilled contributors to group work. His methods were simple but effective, involving building in time for students to de-brief group activities, reflecting and noting examples of their own and one another's **task-maintaining** and **group-maintaining** behaviours.

'Task-maintaining' behaviours were those concerned with getting the job done, such as, giving ideas and suggestions, asking for help and ideas, using and shaping other people's ideas, and evaluating options.

'Group-maintaining' behaviours were those which helped the children get on with one another and work together as a team, and include turn-taking, being cheerful, using humour to defuse conflict, and offering encouragement and praise to other group members.

Thacker describes how this relatively simple intervention elicited increasingly sophisticated insights from the children involved in his studies. He notes the value of providing children with concepts and a language through which to talk about and understand group processes. In his own studies, improved social behaviour and quality of work were evident.

Try to make use of Thacker's ideas in a lesson which you will be delivering shortly. Take time at the beginning to talk through the 'process skills' … the task and group-maintaining behaviours necessary to get the job done, and let the children know that you'll be looking out for these behaviours when they get down to work. Devise a simple pro-forma which the children can use in the last 5–10 minutes of the lesson to rate their own, and other group members' performance with reference to the task and group-maintaining behaviours you have identified as necessary for effective task completion.

For these ideas to work well, it is particularly important to build in plenty of time at the end of the group work activity for review and de-briefing, during which children's attention is drawn toward identifying their learning about their own skills in contributing to the group task, and the ways in which they can plan to use or apply this learning in future group work activities in order to enhance their own and the group's performance.

Conclusion

Awareness of the stages of group development summarised in Figure 3.3 will be helpful in enabling the teacher to craft the group, and steer it through the stages suggested by Tuckman and Jensen 1977.

Stage 1: Forming

- Establish explicit rules and routines from the outset (and reinforce these consistently). Note: The rules should be driven by a framework of values (e.g. respect for others; the need to safeguard all children's rights to work in a calm and happy environment), which are shared with the students, and supported by their parents.
- Communicate positive expectations.
- Organise activities that help students to get to know one another (e.g. via Circle activities).
- Tell students about yourself, particularly the things that you value and/or will not accept in your class.
- Use every available opportunity to use positive performance-related feedback to keep your rules, routines and expectations in students' minds, and to demonstrate that conforming to these pays dividends.
- Work hard at establishing a work-oriented culture:
  - emphasise that the classroom is a work place;
  - ensure that rules and routines are effective in providing an organisational framework which creates a sound climate for learning;
  - make sure that the purpose of tasks and activities is clearly communicated, so that students can easily see the value of the work they do;
  - try to make sure that most of your feedback relates to the specific task and group-maintaining behaviours which you are trying to help the children develop;
  - encourage pupils to try to improve on their own past performance (e.g. in terms of quality of presentation, accuracy, quantity, language usage, level of 'on task' behaviour ...), rather than compare their performance with that of other students. Their task is to make the most of their own capabilities, irrespective of the rate of progress of other students;
  - make use of Circle Time to develop an affiliative, collaborative classroom ethos.

Stage 2: Storming

- When using group work as an integral part of teaching and learning:
  - build in time at the beginning of the activity to clarify the roles and behaviours that will be necessary to get the job done;
  - while students are working, monitor and give formative feedback relating to the quality of these task-related processes and behaviours and, most importantly:
  - allocate plenty of time at the end of the activity, for students to de-brief, and to give and receive feedback re their own and one another's performance, e.g. what skills/behaviours helped get the job done; what skills/behaviours got in the way; how could the group manage a similar task even more efficiently in the future? Encourage the children to consider what they have learned about working as a group/their own skills and limitations as a group member, and to set a target for themselves for the next time they work as a group. This approach helps build students' self-awareness, and gives them a language through which they can increase awareness of the range of roles and behaviours that help a group gel, and work together productively (i.e. to develop high social and task reflexivity).
- Find opportunities to give students feedback on their social roles, to try to avoid rigid, unidimensional 'images' building up. For example, pointing out and valuing examples of 'out of character' behaviour, (such as when the class bully shows skills of leadership or of encouraging others, or when a quiet and conforming student contributes to successful task completion by generating some creative ideas in a brainstorming session), has value:
  - in increasing each child's own awareness of their possibilities;
  - in reinforcing the range of skills and behaviours that contribute to success with work (the task-maintaining roles), and to harmonious relationships (the group-maintaining roles); and
  - in influencing students' perceptions of one another, and making them more aware of one another's many positive characteristics.

Figure 3.3 Managing the social dynamics of the classroom (*continued overleaf*)

- Maintain use of Circle Time further to consolidate affiliation, communication and co-operation, and to trouble-shoot emerging problems.

Keep the rules and routines introduced at the 'forming' stage alive, so that a framework for regulating behaviour remains in place.

- Include explicit age-appropriate work on 'getting along', and interpersonal problem solving in your personal social education programme. Michael Bernard's (1994) 'You Can Do It! Education: Programme Achieve' offers a useful resource which children enjoy, and which explicitly addresses this area. Additionally, Circle Time activities offer a rich seam that can be utilised to support the development of a calm, cooperative, democratic classroom culture.

3: Norming

- If the 'Forming' and 'Storming' stages of the group have been managed successfully, the 'Norming' stage will flow seamlessly from these stages and will simply be a matter of fine tuning and further reinforcement.
- If you are dissatisfied with the norms that are emerging, and conflict-laden or competitive relationships predominate, and/or the classroom climate is simply not work or achievement-oriented, the following steps are suggested:
  - review your classroom management. Are you using a positive, motivational approach? Is the discipline policy effective and being implemented consistently?
  - review the curriculum. Is the work set relevant and interesting and pitched at an appropriate level of difficulty? Is task duration realistic? Are attractive and appropriate resources, and instructional guidance available to support children's learning?
  - are some of the difficulties in the class dynamics a result of problems with individual students? Can the needs of these children be planned for in a more systematic way?
  - if you are satisfied with your classroom management, curriculum delivery and provision for the needs of individual children, including pupils with special educational needs, it will be worth going back to Stages 1 and 2 of this process. Let children know you are unhappy with the classroom dynamics, and why. Invite their cooperation to help solve the problem, (e.g. through Circle Time discussion) and elicit their motivation and commitment by ensuring that they are aware of the advantages to them of making improvements. Then take time to reinforce the rules and routines, to use Circle Time and other small group activities to get students working together, in different combinations.

4: Performing

- Requires only maintenance of norms already established
- If productive norms have not been established, or begin to deteriorate over time, a planful return to the previous stages is recommended (see above).

5: Adjourning

- Schools have a number of successful systems and strategies in place to mark the end of the academic year, and/or children's time at the school. These include:
  - special assemblies and church services;
  - classroom based celebrations;
  - planned de-briefing activities that give children the opportunity to talk and write about their experiences over the year, and to give one another positive feedback about the things they have enjoyed, the personal attributes they have most appreciated and the memories they can take with them and treasure.

These activities serve an important function, helping children to deal with the emotional stress that inevitably accompanies any significant change in their life circumstances.

Figure 3.3   Managing the social dynamics of the classroom

Taking the Tuckman and Jensen model as an example, the practical steps for managing the social dynamics of a newly constituted group shown in Figure 3.3 are recommended. Remember, the group may not progress through these stages in a smooth, sequential flow. The teacher as the manager of the class may need to use Circle activities, and/or the strategies used by Thacker 1990 to help the class reflect on how they are getting along, and to set and review targets in order to achieve more acceptable norms.

Further reading

Bennett, N. (1995) 'Managing learning through Groupwork' in C. Desforges (ed.) *An Introduction to Teaching: Psychological Perspectives.* Oxford: Blackwell.

Curry, M. and Bromfield, C. (1995) *Personal and Social Education for Primary Schools Through Circle Time.* Staffordshire: NASEN Enterprises Ltd.

Stanford, G. (1990) *Developing Effective Classroom Groups.* Bristol: Acorn Group.

CHAPTER 4

De-stressing children in the classroom

Dave Traxson

Introduction

It is hard to define what is meant by stress, as it is a commonly used term meaning many different things to different people; it may be the environmental or psychological demand, the inner state of mind and/or the physical reactions to such pressures. Additionally, as Maurice Chazan points out, (Varma 1996) there can be different levels of stress, and children have a huge range of individual differences in their vulnerability to or ability to cope with adverse events, so it becomes hard to separate out the relationship between cause and effect for any child or group.

A useful psychological definition to set the context for this chapter is that of Tom Cox 1971, who identifies stress as 'arising from any conflict between demand on a person and his ability to cope; or what he thinks a demand is and what he thinks his ability to cope is; an imbalance causes stress'. Lazarus and Folkman's 1984 transactional model highlights that the event, the environment and the individual, through their transactions, determine the stress perceived by the individual. Stress can be increased by other environmental factors like tiredness, background noise, diet, excess movement, air quality, and a whole range of stimuli to the senses. Some children have lower thresholds to any stimulus and this can trigger an excessive response.

An increasing number of educationalists and people working with children in schools feel that the vast majority of pupils with the emotional, behavioural and learning difficulties which are frequently observed in classrooms are acting as they do, not because of some inner deficiency or flaw but because of an accumulation of stressors that are adversely affecting their mental and physical state. This impacts on their ability to concentrate and learn, their views of themselves, their inner happiness and because of this, their relationships with others.

Teachers intuitively know that the more difficult a child is to like and to get on with, the more he needs special care and support but with the escalating demands placed on class teachers these days it is not surprising that some find it hard to motivate themselves to put in this additional effort. It is often easier to motivate class teachers to develop additional support and individual programmes for a child with an academic difficulty, say in learning to read, than to invest energy in a troubled or troublesome child. The aim of this chapter is to present information which will offer constructive and practical help to teacher colleagues to address more of these difficulties, in logical, useful and achievable ways thus benefiting the students they have concerns about and also giving the teachers a greater sense of job satisfaction.

Let us now describe some of the signs of stress in children we work with, before moving on to the causes of the stress and eventually strategies which are useful in class to ameliorate the pressures that children bring into class with them.

Physical and psychological indicators of stress in children

It is useful to be aware of some of the physical and psychological signs of stress that teachers often observe in children in their classes.

Physical:

Regular aches and pains and illness, e.g. colds, etc.

Overheating/sweatiness

Fidgety/constant hand movements

Swallowing/gulping/sighing

Muscular tenseness – facial grimaces

Sucking objects, clothing, etc. Dribbling.

Need for the toilet/toileting problems

Excessive tiredness – either sleepy or edgy/restless

Faster breathing/respiratory problems

More senstive than usual to stimuli

Psychological

Emotional/Behavioural:

Tearful if fails or on separation from parent/friend

Agitated/panic attacks, impulsive

Withdrawn/isolates self physically or by not responding

Poor coordination on tasks they usually can do

Aggressive verbally/physically

Low/depressed, down about self/work. Giving up easily. Resistant to starting tasks/relationships

Bites nails/sucks thumb/picks nose/comfort behaviours

Demands physical contact

Dependent on support/reassurance.

Cognitive/Academic

'I can't do it'. 'Dunno!'

Problem dominated. 'It's all awful!'

Paranoid. 'They're always picking on me!

Poor performance relative to ability, and poor retention

Pessimistic. 'It won't get better'.

Irrational thoughts. 'I can't do well at anything'.

Tongue tied

Misses the point. Misunderstands. Confused

Will not attempt work that he can do

Figure 4.1 Common signs of stress exhibited by children in class

> In Figure 4.1 I have given ten signs of stress for each category. In the three categories list other signs of stress in children that you have noticed or think apply.

Now, before panic sets in, it is normal for all children to manifest some of these signs for some of the time but warning bells should ring if the same child or group of children are showing an unreasonable number of these signs at a significant intensity. These children will need targeting for an individual or group approach to address their worries and stress levels.

Some useful questions for teachers to address in relation to these children in their care are:

- Has there been a very significant increase in physical or health related indicators of stress, e.g. a lot more illness etc. without an apparent medical cause?
- Has there been a sudden and significant increase recently in the behavioural indicators of stress for the child/children the teacher is concerned about?
- Has there been a number of significant life event changes that are contributing to their stress?
- Has there been a significant change in the child's mood, attitude to work and others, motivation and completion of tasks?
- Is the child unaware of the apparent changes and what is his view of the problem?

If the answer to more than one or two of these questions is yes then the teacher will need to discuss the situation with the child and/or his parents in order to help to remedy the situation and to give the child more awareness of and self efficacy about his difficulties.

Anxiety is best viewed as a 'learned or acquired fear' (Mischel 1976). Often it applies to a specific situation but if not addressed might generalise; for example, a child who has ongoing worries about spelling and writing, as they get older might develop a generalised fear about school if the earlier concern is not tackled by the teacher and parents. So anxiety about some situations might contribute to an overall high level of stress with other manifestations, but not necessarily. It is normal for children to have some anxiety/worry about some aspect of school life or the curriculum and children need reassurance when this happens.

Stress and arousal

A certain level of stress or arousal is also normal and healthy and can promote better academic and social achievement; we all need to be challenged to teach or to learn well in a classroom, but as in Figure 4.2, the arousal curve shows that if children become too aroused, stressed, or threatened then they pass a point of optimum performance and dip into a more negative cycle of frustration, failure and negative feelings, which itself then can then sustain low self-esteem and high levels of general anxiety.

It is important to accept that younger children, especially, are not aware that they are suffering from stress, despite sometimes experiencing powerful and painful feelings. It is a responsibility for the adults that care for them, teachers and parents, to notice their reactions and problem-solve ways of best supporting them.

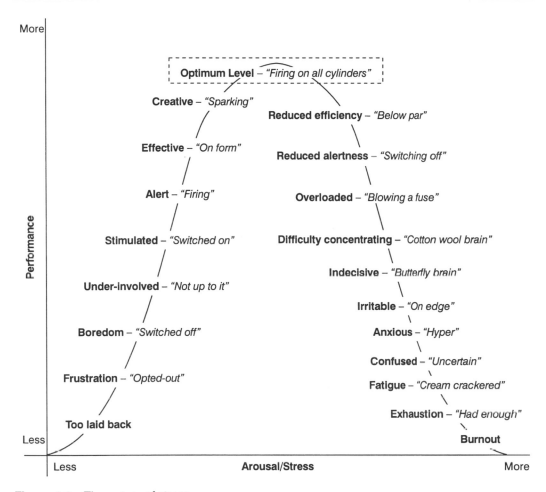

Figure 4.2   The nature of stress

The stress bucket

The stress bucket metaphor has been refined through work with teachers over the years and has proved to be useful to explore the causes of stress with staff, children and parents. It is unlikely that a high level of stress in a child has been brought about by one or two life events, unless they were especially traumatic, such as abuse or involvement in a disaster, and so it is useful to imagine that we all have an imaginary stress bucket in our heads which is never empty – that would not be normal – but into which stress in differing measures accumulates and may eventually overflow. The metaphor evolved as a result of interviewing children in rooms where there is usually a standard issue metal waste basket and everyday items such as teaspoons, cups and bottles to act as visual prompts for the measures, which is helpful when using the strategy as a counselling tool. (See Figure 4.3.)

Using this metaphor does not mean that there is a simple mechanical additive effect which produces the same level of stress in all children, because it is clear that this depends on the interaction with the environment. For example, calmer parents tend to

The
STRESS BUCKET
Metaphor

Some examples of different measures of stress that a child or children are experiencing may be as follows and they can come from either home, outside school or in class. They can be internal (arising from within the child, self-imposed) or external (from outside themselves)

TEASPOONS	CUPFULS	KETTLEFULS
A distant news item or event e.g. famine or war	A local incident, accident or loss	Violence in class or at home
Not sure about/Not liking a piece of work	Finding a piece of work hard	Finding a piece of work impossible
A negative comment to anyone in the child's class	A negative comment to the child	Verbal bullying of child
Wanting something e.g. a toy or outing	Wanting to do well at a task	Wanting to be the 'best' at football (cock of the form)
Not sitting with best friend	Not sitting with any friend	Sitting next to someone whom the child dislikes
'I can't kick a ball'	'I can't do this homework'	'I can't do anything'
Breaking a pencil	Forgetting equipment	Cannot afford a pen
No money for tuck	No money for school trip	Parent unemployed
Seeing a scary cartoon	Watching a realistic war film	Watching a pornographic video
'I must be on time for my mother'	'I must *always* be on time'	'I must go to school even when I'm sick'
Food additives e.g. in crisps at tuck shop	Caffeine in drinks e.g. cola	No breakfast regularly or totally inappropriate diet
One bad night's sleep	Regular bad nights' sleep	Staying up to 2–3 am to watch a horror film

Figure 4.3   The stress bucket

reduce the stress in their children, thus helping them cope better and the personality variables in the child will also greatly affect this. The process of using the stress bucket as a counselling tool, to listen to the child's views or with a group, is relevant and should be of practical use to teachers when having a one-to-one chat with a child to whom they are giving support.

It is useful to start with some prompts using objects in the physical environment, if possible, and to explain that everyone has one of these stress or worry buckets in their head, including their parents, friends and even their teachers and to normalise their feelings about this. At any one time there are stresses going into our bucket that are of different sizes, thus the spoon, cup and kettle or jug (equivalent measures can obviously be used). By some self-disclosure or giving general examples that affect children of their age the onus is then shifted to the child to talk about their own experience and feelings at the moment. It is a safe process and the child remains in control and they will only share views that they are prepared to, depending on the level of trust they have with the adult involved.

> When and how would you use the stress bucket metaphor with an individual child or group of children in your classroom? Would you feel comfortable using it one-to-one in an interview? How would you approach talking to a child about the stresses they are experiencing in an age appropriate way?

The examples children give are not neatly graded like those in Figure 4.3 but these have been chosen to illustrate the relative intensity and size of typical stressors.

This model also recognises individual differences and notions of thresholds. To one child a kettleful may be a stressor but to another a cupful, and some children may have a bigger bucket to start with. One key point though, is that in the end it does not matter, when the bucket overflows, whether a teaspoon or a kettleful went in last, *it is overflowing* and the information provided might give us useful insights into how to best help the child to bail out some stress by the coping strategies they use.

The pro-forma in Appendix 4.1 can be used to facilitate the discussion with a child.

In some children the bucket overflowing will manifest itself as a sudden and violent, 'fight or flight' reaction where the levels of adrenalin circulating in the child are such that this well-established biological reflex action is triggered and a 'red rage' or running away ensues. We, as educators, need to be proactive in predicting a child who is getting agitated in this way and anticipate the need to provide a 'safe place' or 'key person' where the child can go in order to calm down so that they will then be able to react more rationally to a teacher who may try to talk through their difficulties. We might choose to involve the child in monitoring their own levels of agitation, and response to provocation. For example, the child showing a yellow card when their level is rising and a red card when they feel they need to leave the class to calm down: the football analogy can be motivating!

The success cycle to help ameliorate stresses

Another very important interaction is between the child's level of stress and their self-esteem. Self-esteem is the power behind the production of lasting change and also the reduction of anxiety. A positive view of themselves can reduce significantly the impact of stresses in the child's life, especially if the child feels they have some control over the factors influencing them and choices available to them. Teachers and parents have a vital role in oiling the wheels of the success cycle (see Figure 4.4).

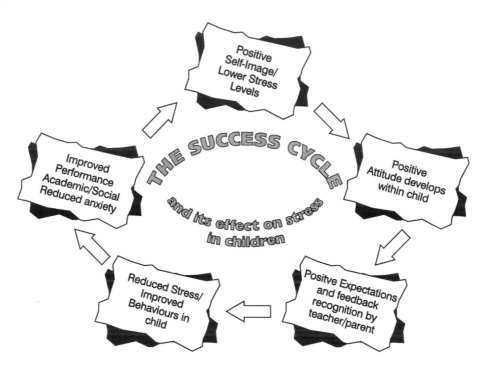

Figure 4.4   The wheel which teachers and parents can oil

It is clear from a wide range of studies and approaches that a class teacher's role in this process is vital and the selective, specific and high quality positive recognition or validation which is given in a way which is meaningful to the child is the 'engine house' of achieving a permanent change in a child's level of stress and performance. Relative progress in a social skill should always be recognised as a way of achieving more in the future, rather than expecting an absolute change e.g. you should *always* behave like this.

Thus, a child who starts to achieve five minute bursts of calm concentration on their work needs to have this recognised as a way of developing that particular skill. If we miss these opportunities we miss the chance to achieve lasting change, by shaping up appropriate behaviours.

Teachers do have an essential role in helping children to develop their emotional intelligence as well as their cognitive abilities. 'Emotional Intelligence' (Goleman 1996) includes a child being:

- aware of their feelings and expressing them;
- managing their feelings and reactions better;
- controlling impulses more effectively (self-control);

- reducing their stress by reducing uncertainty and setting realistic objectives and also helping them to set realistic objectives for themselves;
- using positive self-talk and problem-solving to replace problems and develop their effective communication skills.

> How could you shape up the use of appropriate coping strategies in children and give expectations that build self-esteem and reduce their levels of uncertainty or stress?

Children who cope better

According to Saunders 1984, children who are likely to cope effectively with stress display more features of being 'A Capable Kid' (see extract below, reproduced with permission of Multimedia Product Development, Chicago, Il.)

A 'Capable Kid' is:

Spontaneous	Active, energetic	Happy
Reflective	Thoughtful	Physically affectionate
Willing to take risks	Likes himself	Helpful
Cooperative	Has good eye contact	Has a sense of humour
Seeks help readily	Owns up to mistakes	Has goals and ambitions
Resourceful	Confident/assertive	Relaxed
Able to express feelings	Capable of being excited about good things	

She suggests that the key aspects of helping children to deal with stress is giving them validation and a sense of security. Validation means giving them the feeling that they are 'doing all right' and are lovable people, and security is achieved by consistently showing we are there for them and communicating with them honestly and openly. This relates also to Maslow's Hierarchy of Needs (1943) referred to in Chapter 1 as when a child feels safe and has a sense of being loved and belonging their self-esteem is enhanced and this helps them to self-actualise, fulfilling their potential. The feeling of being valued as a person and having unique contributions/skills is the key that teachers and parents turn to unlock the potential that is within all children, despite it sometimes being hidden. This in turn enables them to cope better with the demands placed on them.

> How would you set about validating children i.e. valuing the strengths of children in your class who are stressed and engendering a sense of belonging to the whole class?

Children's reaction to trauma

Different children can experience the same disaster or trauma e.g. a bodily reaction produced by a wound, external violence or emotional shock) very differently which is likely to be related to how much self-confidence, ability to control their environment and locus of control they have. In Weisaeth's 1993 view, 'the subjects' responses during the impact phase, and how they viewed them in the aftermath deeply affected the type and intensity of their past traumatic reactions'.

According to Houghton 1996 there are certain 'types' of children who need to be more carefully monitored in the event of a disaster/trauma. These include:

- children with special educational needs who may react more severely;
- boys, who are less likely to talk about their experiences;
- children who have not resolved earlier losses/shocks;
- children who have been physically or sexually abused previously;
- children with emotional difficulties and who are naturally more vulnerable;
- children who have difficulty using existing support systems.

Naturally, the corollary of this is that more confident, socially and academically skilled individuals who have been lucky enough to avoid significant loss or harm are significantly less at risk following a disaster.

As the last point in the above list indicates, schools provide stability and a vital continuity to children, indeed sometimes schools are the most stable aspect of their lives. It is essential that they provide a supportive, stable and caring response especially to the 'at risk' groups following a disaster. Some children, even those 'at risk', might not show features that we would expect and even sometimes an opposite pattern, due to the confused state they are in. To assist healthy adjustment to a traumatic event the victim has to come to terms with and to assimilate what has happened to them. Yule 1991 emphasises that for this to be possible, the child must be helped to make sense of what has happened and to gain understanding and control over their feelings. He developed 'Critical Incident Stress Debriefing' techniques for this purpose, as did Dyregrov 1993 in Norway.

Best and Mead 1998 in their excellent chapter, identify seven aspects of adjustment that need to be understood and recognised before a suitable intervention can be utilised with a child or group of children. The aspects are shown in Figure 4.5.

They also identify the most useful model describing the effects of trauma or grief and mourning as that of Baker and Duncan 1992 which has been adapted to include the levels of communication involved as shown in Figure 4.6.

This is not a linear sequence that children neatly pass through but teachers should expect to see some progression through these natural stages and this allows them to tell the child that what they are experiencing is normal and to be expected, without minimising the significance of the child's own feelings and bodily reactions. This can be reassuring to children and staff alike.

The first tier of support should always be people that are well known to the children, which is why teachers and parents should be helped to give the best support they can to the children in the first place. Outside support is useful in the early stages at a consultancy level but usually should only be used directly with individual children

Communication Level	Aspect of Adjustment	Signs associated with it
Head	Cognitive	– e.g. confusion, sequencing difficulties, indecisiveness, poor concentration, loss of memory/judgement, decline in functioning
	Psychological	– e.g. obsessive behaviour, loss of concentration, personality change, increased dreams/nightmares, fear of recurrence, very protective to others
Heart	Emotional	– e.g. need to be cared for, sad, anxious, anger or guilt feelings
Body	Behavioural	– Sudden changes e.g. clingyness, regression, obsessive talk, loss of self-control, substance abuse etc.
	Physical	– e.g. headaches, shivering, tiredness, loss of appetite (see list)
	Practical	– e.g. inability to cope with routines at home or school
Soul	Spiritual	– e.g. new or renewed faith/beliefs or loss of faith

Figure 4.5   Adapted from Best and Mead's (1998) seven aspects of adjustment

Loss to 2 months after incident	Shock	— Physical/Mental
	Numbness	— Depersonalisation/withdrawal etc.
	Denial	— 'It can't be true'
1–3 months and ongoing after	Anxiety	— Irrational fears, increased dependency
	Guilt	— Self-recriminations
	Anger	— 'Why me?'/Misplaced anger
	Grief	— Pain
	Loneliness	— Rejection/Emptiness
	Yearning	— Nightmares, self-interest etc.
	Searching	— Wanting it as it was, looking for solution
8–9 months and ongoing after	Depression	— Despair, mood dips, anxiety etc.
	Apathy	— Lack of will, denial, neglects self and friends
	Loss of identity	— 'Who am I now?'
	Stigma	— Possible labelling
	Motivation	— Rediscovery of old self if grieving
1–2 years after and ongoing	Acceptance	— Settling more, regains interests
	Healing	— Restructures life, regains balance, more mature

Figure 4.6   Effects of trauma. Adapted from Baker and Duncan (1992)

or classes if there is an extreme reaction, or if the child/children are stuck for long periods in the early stages e.g. experiencing denial, anger and shock, six months later. This would be immobilising for a child. All people have a quota or parcel of energy to utilise emotionally and if this is used up unproductively on repressing feelings or thinking irrational and negative thoughts then nothing is left or not enough energy is left to cope with the expected demands at that time and mental health or physical problems might follow. Interacting with this are the age and maturity of the child at the time of a trauma and the effect on cognitive development and skills, so a younger child is likely, normally, to take longer to come to terms with a significant loss or trauma than a teenager.

School based strategies to help children

Regardless of the scale of the disaster/trauma or a child's individual stresses there are certain stages to a supportive and healing process that are necessary.

> In your experience what events have constituted a crisis in the children you have worked with and would following this sequence have been helpful?

The worst thing adults can do is to avoid making contact with the children personally and avoid talking about the trauma or stresses. The child or children would feel rejected at a time when human contact, love and interest are vital. Teachers and staff with the support of outside agencies like educational psychologists need to review their actions and refine them on the basis of the learning that has occurred and the advice that has been offered. Staff should only act in ways that they feel comfortable with and if they feel out of their depth, support should be readily available.

Approaches for individual children in class
- Build a better knowledge of/relationship with the child.
- Listen to the child more. Accept their feelings and pain.
- Use media other than talking e.g. creative writing, feelings diaries, self-monitoring sheets, poetry, and drawing.
- Use a problem-solving approach (see Appendix 4.2). Help them to see how they could move toward a better tomorrow (see Appendix 4.3 – 'Self-planner for a better future/INSPIRE model').
- Develop and use a 'cooling off' strategy with a child or a 'safe place', 'safe person' strategy.
- Use Learning Conversations (see Chapter 5).
- Set up 'buddy' systems and peer tutoring programmes with another trusted child giving support to the student you are concerned about.
- Use a higher rate of praise with a child you are concerned about (children need three times as much praise as criticism).
- Involve a colleague with specialist skills or a member of a support team.
- Involve volunteer parents to help boost a child's academic skill level.

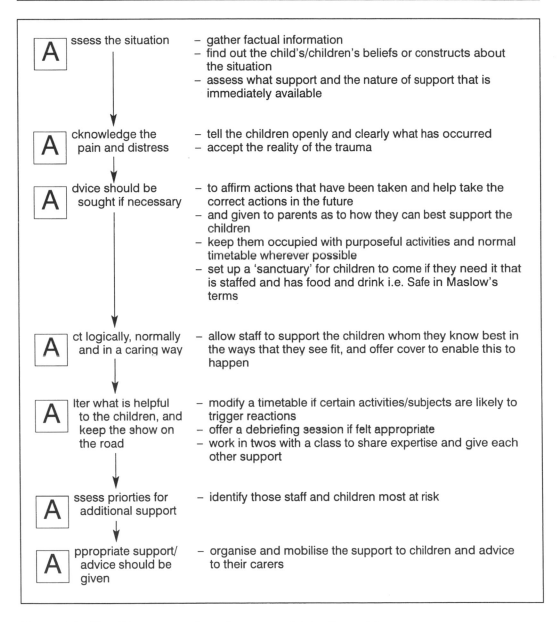

Figure 4.7 The 7A's sequence for acting appropriately after a crisis

- Have clear routines and punctuate your lesson/day – routines create security and reduce uncertainty.
- Train the child in an Emergency Stop technique STOP – Take Three Deep Breaths – Think what you will positively achieve – then resume work.
- Teach and support the child in using more advanced relaxation techniques e.g. progressive muscular relaxation.
- Teach the child to recognise and record their signs of stress e.g. use a self monitoring card with a 1–10 rating for stress levels.

- Teach the child to be more assertive in their response to situations.
- Reinforce, specifically praise and encourage any improvement in their coping behaviour.
- Use stressproofing strategies for the child (Markham 1996).
- Use the Calmer Plan Sheet (Appendix 4.4) with the child.

Strategies to reduce or prevent stresses in groups or classes

- Be there for them – children know when adults care and are being supportive.
- Change the atmosphere/ambience.
- Use a naturally relaxing essential oil like lavender.
- Use soothing music as a background for children to work more calmly.
- Develop or use a commercially available stress management package, such as 'How to De-stress Your Child' Saunders 1984.
- Use Circle Time (see Chapter 3) as a daily routine to encourage positive recognition of people's strengths.
- Use group work in a cross-curricular way or in a specific therapeutic way to discuss and work on common skills and issues that affect the group.
- Try some social skills training by targeting specific skills the children need to develop such as good manners or being cooperative or by following a commercial package like *Teaching Students to Get Along* (Canter 1997).
- Use accreditation schemes which recognise achievement e.g. the Youth Award Scheme (ASDAN) or Club 2000 (Chris Traxson 1998).
- Use Group Relaxation Techniques such as 'guided imagery'.
- Use group meditation e.g. the Benson technique where the group in chorus repeat a neutral word or 'mantra'.
- Have class pets for children to look after.
- Build up the whole group or small group identity by fostering working as a team.
- Use drama and role play to deal with children's fears and anxieties in a safe way.
- Develop their confidence in talking in a group by regular 'show and tell' sessions.
- Use a Peer Support Model where a child volunteers to share a concern and then the discussion is led by the teacher through the stages of:

Elaboration   (Finding out as much information as possible about the
   ↓   concern)

Prioritising   (Selecting which aspects to act on)
   ↓
Solution Finding   (Brainstorm possible options)
   ↓
Intervening   (Try out the one you like)

- Reduce background noise by having a 'noise monitor' who indicates by some signal e.g. standing up, that everyone needs to turn down the volume.
- Developing turn taking.
- Use story telling and performed music as a way of punctuating the day.

Which of these strategies would you feel most comfortable using with either individuals or groups of children and what support would you need?

Further reading

Alsop, P. and McCaffrey, T. (1993). *How to Cope with Childhood Stress*. Harlow: Longman.

Kleber, R. and Brom, D. (1992) *Coping with Trauma. Theory, Prevention and Treatment*. London: Jessica Kingsley.

Leaman, O. (1996) Death and Loss – Compassionate Approaches in the Classroom. London: Cassell.

Romsberg, B. and Saunders, A. (1984) *Help your Child Cope with Stress*. London: Piatkus.

Varma, V. (ed.) (1996) *Coping with Children in Stress*. Aldershot: Arena/Ashgate.

CHAPTER 5

Exploring pupil motivation and promoting effective learning in the classroom

Paul Timmins

Introduction

All teachers encounter poorly motivated pupils and most will have experienced the frustration of having their best efforts to support and encourage ignored or seemingly rejected. For many of these pupils, the way in which they have come to construe classroom activities is often confused, stemming from an inadequate ability to understand and plan their work and to act on teacher feedback and guidance. This poor task-related thinking and performance is not necessarily associated with a lack of ability but is often more a function of poor habits of mind. This chapter introduces methods teachers can use to explore pupils' thinking about tasks and as a consequence reveal reasons for poor motivation. It also describes ways in which pupils can learn effective 'learning how to learn' strategies.

Understanding poorly motivated pupils

The examples presented below illustrate ways in which pupils 'get it wrong' and as a consequence experience failure in the classroom. Pupils' beliefs about the tasks represented are so firmly held that they are unable to respond to commonly available levels of teacher feedback which aim to improve performance and motivation. A structured, psychological approach to uncovering the reasons for these difficulties led to an understanding of the reasons for their persistent failure and allowed for appropriate support to be provided. Many of the techniques used to identify and overcome these difficulties are described in this chapter.

- A young pupil with a puzzlingly slow rate of handwriting believed that what his teacher valued in his written work was his ability to create equal spaces between words, rather than the content of his writing.
- Another pupil responded to his teacher's exhortation to work hard at his written work by putting extreme effort into forming individual letters in words, rather than into its content.

- One obviously bright eight year old, reading at the six year level startled her teachers with the extent to which she misunderstood what she read. Sensitive monitoring of the process she used to abstract meaning from the text showed that she constructed meaning by consciously focusing on the words she knew she could not read, guessing at these and using her guesses as a basis for constructing the meaning of the text. She rarely focused her attention on the meaning of the words she could read accurately in the text to build comprehension.

- A bright sixteen year old reading like a seven year old believed that successful readers read words with 100 per cent accuracy and had 100 per cent comprehension and recall of material read. These beliefs contributed to her sense of failure and lack of motivation. (As she read at her level, she made mistakes and forgot some of what she had read.) Formative reading experiences in the home included having to learn parts of religious texts by heart, which may have accounted for her beliefs about the process of reading.

> Without knowledge of why these pupils were failing to make progress, how do you feel teachers would respond to these pupils in the context of their everyday teaching, in their main areas of difficulty? In what sense might these responses be of help or hindrance to the pupil concerned?

Attribution theory: understanding pupils' thinking about success and failure

Attribution theory assumes that pupils and indeed all learners try to understand why they succeed or fail. The theory suggests that attributions or reasons for success or failure are construed by learners along the dimensions described in Figure 5.1. Causes may be construed as stemming from internal factors such as ability or effort or external causes such as task difficulty and luck. Each of these dimensions is also considered to be either stable or unstable. The relationships between these are shown in Figure 5.1 with examples of how each type of pupil attribution might explain poor performance on a maths test.

	SOURCE OF CAUSE	
	INTERNAL	**EXTERNAL**
Stable cause	**Ability** 'I'm hopeless at Maths.'	**Task difficulty** 'That test was really hard and much too long.'
Unstable cause	**Effort** 'I should have revised more instead of watching T.V.'	**Luck** 'What bad luck, all the questions came from lessons I missed'

Figure 5. Attribution theory and the causes of success and failure. Adapted from Developmental Psychology, 4th Ed., by D.R. Shaffer 1996. Reprinted with permission of Wadsworth Publishing, a division of International Thomson Publishing. Fax 0800 730-2215.

The figure shows that pupils who tend to attribute their poor performance to their low ability (stable cause, tending not to be modifiable) rather than effort (unstable and modifiable) are unlikely to believe that they can change their performance on a task they have failed on; whereas pupils who have failed but feel they have not put enough effort in are likely to respond to encouragement to try harder (to increase effort, which is modifiable).

How to encourage positive attributions

Teachers can encourage effort and avoid discouraging pupils by ensuring that the feedback they give to pupils supports the development of positive attributions.

Borich and Tombari 1995, p. 234 suggest that comments which:

- express sympathy at failure
- show surprise at success
- give excessive unsolicited help
- lavishly praise success on easy tasks

are all likely to suggest that pupils have low ability.

These authors suggest that comments which possess the qualities described below encourage pupils to feel that effort is rewarded by success and also support the development of effective learning strategies. In these examples, clear and accurate feedback is given on the strategies pupils use to complete tasks as well as the outcomes achieved. Criticism alone or even faint praise and sympathy may suggest that pupils lack ability.

These messages:

- Are directed at a pupil's actions, not at his or her character or person. *'Your answers show thought.'* **Not:** *'You are a good thinker.'*
- Reflect an accurate or honest evaluation of pupil performance. *'Your answers to these questions are too brief and need to show more thought. The other answers are thorough, thoughtful; and show understanding of the material.'* **Not:** *'Some of your answers are fantastic. All of them show real effort.'* **And not:** *'I feel bad that you got such a low grade.'*
- Help pupils believe in themselves and their own ability. *'Your handwriting's much improved. I appreciate the effort you're putting into it.'* **Not** *'Here's a smiley face for that neat work.'*
- Attribute pupil achievement to internal rather than external factors. *'You have good ideas; you should want people to understand them. That's why it's important to write clearly.'* **Not:** *'Write grammatically correct sentences or else I'll take off a point for each mistake.'*

Adapted from Borich and Tombari 1995, p. 234

What attributional information is conveyed to pupils by the types of feedback statement you use most frequently in your classroom?

This section has provided insights into ways in which teachers might relate to pupils in everyday teaching contexts and examples of how to support positive thinking about classroom tasks. The section below builds on this and describes more direct processes for exploring and influencing pupil's attributions and improving task motivation and performance.

Developing metacognitive skills: helping pupils to become aware of the thinking associated with successful learning

Children who have metacognitive awareness have the capacity to plan how best to tackle a variety of tasks and through reviewing their efforts are able to improve their future plan-making capacity and therefore their effectiveness as learners. Metacognitive skills can be taught and support a lifelong learning perspective which, in its most powerful form, anticipates that learners will transfer 'learning how to learn' skills acquired in educational contexts to work, leisure and social contexts. This section presents a number of approaches which teachers can use to enable pupils to develop control over their own learning and which promote intrinsic or self-directed motivation.

Self-instruction

Self-instruction, as described by McCormick and Pressley 1997, encourages pupils to become aware of the thinking necessary for them to complete tasks successfully. They are taught to use the stages presented below to help them plan and review their approach to tasks. The approach is designed to help pupils to develop the necessary attitudes towards a task. ('*If I plan how I'm going to tackle the task and think hard about the difficulties I anticipate and do something about them, I'm likely to do well!*'). The level of awareness promoted by the plan-making aspect of self-instruction reduces the likelihood that distractions will impair performance and achievement. The stages are:

- Define the problem or task to be addressed.
- Construct a plan to address this.
- Implement the plan and verbalise actions carried out. (Thus, ensuring that the plan is followed.)
- Verbalise difficulties encountered during implementation and any corrective action to be taken.
- Self-reinforce and describe successful plan-related activity while completing the task and later while reviewing performance on it.

The teacher introduces the approach by first demonstrating it in the context of a particular task and then supporting the pupil in its use on the same task. Demonstration involves talking aloud and explaining how the steps in the self-instruction approach are used to make a plan to address the problem and subsequently how to work to the plan. When pupils are confident in using the approach, overt verbalisation can give way to quietly thinking their way through plan making and the management of their own actions as they complete the task.

This approach has been used successfully to help pupils of various ages and abilities to improve: attention to tasks; the amount and quality of written work and to understand and use a variety of procedures which help develop basic educational skills.

Identify a particular skill you wish all pupils in your class to acquire and devise a means of using self-instruction to teach this. How might you involve pupils in giving you feedback on the success of their use of the self-instruction approach and the extent to which the target skill is acquired?

Attunement strategy

This method is described by Hastings 1992 and has been used successfully with underachieving, inattentive and passive pupils who have developed strategies such as queuing or sharpening pencils in order to avoid activities set by their teachers. The attunement strategy lends itself to use during a wider variety of classroom activities than the self-instruction approach. As part of the attunement approach specific types of questions are used to help a pupil to construct a plan to tackle a task. The activity is then carried out and finally teacher and pupil conduct a brief review of the progress made.

At the planning stage, the teacher first elicits the pupil's ideas on how the given task should be tackled and then helps the pupil to make a more appropriate plan if the goals or timescales identified are unrealistic. The following questions are useful at the planning stage:

- What is it that needs to be done, what is the task?
- What goals are to be attained and what is a reasonable time to allow for the work to be completed in? (e.g. how much work will be produced in how much time?)
- How will these goals be achieved, what actions/materials/approaches will be necessary?
- How hard does the pupil think the task likely to be and will it require hard work to complete?
- Will the work be interesting?

This planning conversation need last no longer than a few minutes and should include discussion of ways of overcoming any difficulties identified.

When the time the pupil set for completing the activity has passed, the teacher conducts a brief review. The following questions are useful.

- To what extent were the goals achieved?
- Was the plan to address the goals successful?
- What improvements could be made?
- Was it as difficult as you thought?

In this phase of the discussion, the teacher draws the pupil's attention to progress made and how this was achieved. This enables the pupil to be aware of the effects of the plan in action and helps promote a sense of competence and control over learning. These appreciations strengthen a pupil's attributions relating to the importance of effort as a means of overcoming difficulties and inhibit a tendency to believe that task performance and outcomes are due largely to ability or luck.

Hastings' initial research data on the use of the attunement strategy in 12 primary classrooms showed that targeted pupils' on-task behaviour improved from 35 per cent to 55 per cent, over a period of three weeks.

How would you train all pupils in your class to use the attunement strategy? What effect do you feel the approach would have on pairs of pupils and their ability to help each other to plan and review classroom activities? How could you measure the impact of the attunement strategy on pupils' work output and on their work planning and review skills?

The Salmon Line: exploring pupils' attributions and learning strategies

The Salmon Line devised by Salmon 1988 can be used with individuals or groups to:

- explore the way they understand and view any aspect of school life, and themselves in relation to the school;
- reveal how they feel they learn best and have progressed in relation to a particular topic or subject;
- reveal their beliefs concerning the personal qualities associated with success and failure within a topic;
- provide useful insights into their theories about themselves as learners prior to the use of the self-instruction or attunement approaches.

The information gained from the Salmon Line makes an important contribution to the assessment of motivation and a pupil's favoured approach to learning and as a result allows for teaching and support to be tuned to the needs of the pupil. The approach frequently reveals disabling myths developed by pupils concerning their learning and misinformed processes relating to goal setting and the actions typically carried out to achieve these.

Whatever aspect of school life is chosen for exploration, it is represented as a continuum with one end representing the best or most accomplished one could be in the area under consideration and the other the worst or least accomplished one could possibly be. A conversation between pupil and teacher then focuses on the implications for the pupil of being at different points on this continuum.

Pupils need to be involved in any decision-making stemming from discussion of the results of Salmon Line as this is empowering and helps ensure that plans are perceived to be viable and thought likely to be successful.

The example provided in Figure 5.2 shows how the Salmon Line can be used to explore an individual pupil's thinking about the nature of reading, and their beliefs concerning past, present and future progress in reading.

The Salmon Line can also be used to help teachers understand how a group or class of pupils perceive their levels of competence in relation to a topic or subject, or indeed themselves as learners. For example Salmon Lines could be used to explore pupils' thinking along dimensions such as Good at Maths vs Bad at Maths; Good Learners vs Poor Learners or even Good Behaviour vs Poor Behaviour. Teachers can also complete and compare their Salmon Line results with those of their pupils, discussing reasons for any differences.

1. Draw and then explain the meaning of the continuum for the pupil. (See above)

O————————————————————————————————O

    Poor reader   Good reader

2. Ask the pupil to give their view of the qualities and attributes possessed by the sort of person represented by each end of the continuum. Record these responses at each end of continuum.
(These Responses provide insights into the way the pupil (p) judges success and why they may be failing.)

3. Then ask p to mark the line to show on the reading continuum:
   • Where they feel they are at present.
   • Where they were one year ago.
   • Where they would like to be in a term's time.
   • Their ideal position.

4. Then explore p's beliefs and explanations concerning their movement from position to position along the line using the questions given below.

Sometimes the beliefs elicited will appear rigid and unrealistic and explain poor motivation and learning outcomes. If so, more realistic alternatives need to be introduced.

   • What helped p to move to their current position from a position closer to the poor reader pole?
   (Reveals beliefs about reasons for progress.)
   • What would help p to move to the positions marked for a term's time and their ideal position?
   (Helps with an understanding of beliefs about support necessary for future learning).
   • What can p do now that they couldn't do a year and then a term ago, in relation to reading?
   • What do they feel they will be able to do in a term's time and at their ideal point?
   (These questions help reveal the dimensions p uses to judge their success and the learning outcomes they have in mind.).

Figure 5.2   Using the Salmon Line

Which topics/subjects would it be interesting for you to explore with your pupils using the Salmon Line in the context of your current work in the classroom? How would you ensure that the goals and strategies revealed were transformed into realistic targets and approaches? How could you support pupils and ensure that they monitored their progress towards these? How would you know this initiative had been successful and how would you monitor its progress and evaluate its success?

The theory of Self-Organised Learning (SOL)

This approach is described by Harri-Augstein and Webb 1995 and provides a rich and practical conceptual framework which enables learners to understand their learning processes and to develop the skills associated with learning how to learn. The self-organised learner stands in contrast to the pupil/adult who is overly dependent on others for prescriptions for learning and fails to see the connection between their own activity and thinking and the products of their efforts. Self-organisation, as defined within the theory of SOL, may be attained through reflective planning and review in a diverse range of daily activities. These include parenting, sports and professional activities such as teaching and management as well as through pupils' school-related work. The approach recognises that learning is life-long and that there are opportunities for learning to become self-organised in all everyday activities.

Within SOL, a well defined process called the Learning Conversation (l-c) supports the learner's progress towards self-organisation. This helps the learner to become aware of the thoughts, feelings and actions which they anticipate will lead to desirable outcomes in relation to a particular activity. Then after carrying out the activity, the l-c supports learner reflection on the thoughts, feelings and actions which either contributed to or hindered effectiveness on the task. Learner self-management of the l-c is a skill which requires a 'coach' whose role is to support the learner in the particular plan making and review processes associated with the l-c. The coach needs to be adept at recognising when the learner's motivation for planning or reviewing action is flagging and be able to use the l-c framework to explore reasons for this and to provide the necessary support to continue planning action through the l-c process.

Self-organisation is not attained through a single l-c. A number of l-cs need to be conducted with the support of the coach, preferably within a single topic, before the l-c process is internalised by the learner and can be used without support. In classrooms, for routine activities, pairs of pupils can take it in turns to coach each other. For more complex tasks, where a pupil experiences great difficulty with a particular activity, the teacher may need to act as coach in order to ensure the necessary degree of support.

The l-c begins with the coach helping the learner to identify a topic or domain for learning (learning how to get better at Maths) and within this a particular task (subtracting tens and units). In the case of school related l-cs, pupils will usually require the support of their teacher to identify the topic and task, though plan-making to address the task should be largely under the control of the pupil.

The grid presented in Figure 5.3 was developed by the authors of the theory of SOL (Harri-Augstein and Thomas 1991) to support coach and learner in the use of the l-c process. Each column reflects a phase of the l-c, these being planning the activity in terms of anticipated purposes, methods and outcomes; implementing the plan and noting how it works out in practice, then reviewing its strengths and weaknesses. The review is most effective when conducted before the learner's memory of the actions undertaken begins to fade. This can happen unless some simple form of diary is maintained. It is essential to ensure the review takes place as this helps the learner to develop the ability to learn from experience and to develop a 'learning-how-to-learn' orientation to tasks. Wherever possible, learners should be encouraged to record their own plans and the results of their review on the grid.

Appendix 5.1 presents an adapted version of Harri-Augstein and Thomas' grid, suitable for use in the classroom. It is also accompanied by further notes on the introduction of SOL to the classroom and an example of an l-c and completed grid.

The theory of SOL also identifies types of 'Personal Learning Myths' which may influence a pupil's motivation and capacity for learning. The structure of the l-c

	What are my purposes?	What purposes were reflected in what I actually did?	Describe any differences
Purposes	Elicit purposes learner associates with the selected task	(See Note 1. below)	(See Note 2. below)
Strategies (Actions/ methods)	**What actions shall I take to address my purposes?** Elicit the actions the learner expects to carry out in order to address the purposes identified above. Preparation necessary before this action can be carried out might also be recorded. Actions should be given for each major purpose identified above. Some younger pupils find it easier to begin the l-c by describing the actions they will carry out, rather than their purposes	**What did I actually do?** (See Note 1. below)	**Describe any differences** (See Note 2. below)
Outcomes	**How shall I judge my success?** For each major purpose listed above, elicit the outcome the learner expects to achieve; as a measurable quantity and if possible the qualities the product should have or is expected to have. Finally, check learner's confidence that plan will be pursued and will be successful. Explore reasons for any concerns and adjust plan accordingly	**How well did I actually do?** (See Note 1. below)	**Describe any differences** (See Note 2. below)

What are my strengths?	What are my weaknesses?
Elicit and record these based on information in grid, especially column 3.	Elicit and record these based on information in grid, especially column 3.

Note 1: To complete this column, encourage the learner to reconstruct how they actually went about the activity as if their actions were captured on film. Help them to re-live the actual thinking and feeling driving and guiding this behaviour. This information can be used to reconstruct the activity in terms of the actual purposes driving the actions, actual actions carried out and outcomes actually obtained. These features are entered in the appropriate cells of this column.

Note 2: In this column the learner explains and briefly records the reasons for any differences between the first and second column entries. This information helps the learner construct fresh awareness of the demands of the task and allows for better planning for future work on it. A new and more effective plan can then be made for a similar task using the l-c framework and a new grid. Through this process of review, learners become aware of actions and processes which lead to successful outcomes and learn how to learn.

Figure 5.3 Personal learning contract

provides an opportunity for these to emerge and be challenged by the learning coach and learner.

Myths may concern learners' beliefs about:

- Their own abilities and how these influence their learning. ('I've got a poor memory and so I can't … ' or 'I'm no good at …')
- The conditions under which they learn best. ('I can't work after 8 p.m. unless I'm listening to my favourite music.')
- The way in which particular tasks should be tackled and personal constructions of standards against which one's performance is judged. (See examples given in the section above entitled 'Understanding poorly motivated pupils.)

SOL can be seen as a useful practical extension of Attribution theory in that attributions and beliefs are explored and if necessary challenged within the context of particular classroom or life activities using the l-c process. The Salmon Line and Attunement strategy each provide useful approaches to the exploration of a learner's beliefs and may be used by the coach as part of the l-c to guide planning and review.

Learning how to learn is an important life-long learning skill and teachers need to help pupils to develop this skill. If pupils are not given opportunities to discuss how they tackle activities and the relative merits of approaches used, they will not be proficient at learning from their experience of learning. Support for poorly motivated pupils is often provided by teachers in the form of an instruction to change their style of engagement with a task or to work more quickly. This 'support' is often given without sufficient exploration of the planning and thinking which results in the unsatisfactory outcomes observed. Learning conversations surface pupils' thinking and help them re-construct their approach and achieve better results.

Conducted over-time, l-cs, supported by a teacher or other pupils, enhance movement towards self-organisation. Where learners are not encouraged to plan and review their activity, they will not develop in this manner and their appreciation of themselves as learners will be constructed out of loosely appreciated strategies gleaned from the myriad of methods experienced in the classroom as part of a history as 'other-organised' rather than self-organised learners.

Consider how you might teach pupils to work in pairs to carry out l-cs. What types of activities lend themselves to this planning process and how would you judge the success of your experiment?

This chapter has addressed the reasons why pupils fail in the classroom and has provided techniques teachers may use to help identify the causes of poor motivation and strengthen pupils' capacities as learners. The processes described may be taught to groups of pupils so they can learn to coach and support each other.

Further reading

Croll, P. and Hastings, N. (1996) *Effective Primary Teaching: Research Based Classroom Strategies.* London: David Fulton Publishers.

Harri-Augstein, E. and Webb, I. *(1995) Learning to Change.* London: McGraw-Hill.

McCormick, C. and Pressley, M. (1997) *Educational Psychology: Learning, Instruction and Assessment.* New York: Longman.

Nixon, J., Martin, J., Ranson, S. and McKeown, P. (1996) *Encouraging Learning: Towards a Theory of the Learning School.* Buckingham: Open University Press.

Salmon, P. (1995) *Psychology in the Classroom.* London: Cassell Education.

Whitaker, P. (1995) *Managing to Learn: Aspects of Reflective and Experiential Learning in Schools.* London: Cassell.

CHAPTER 6

Conclusions: using psychology as a basis for action

Jane Leadbetter

Introduction

By now, if you are reading this chapter you will have read some or all of the book and will be considering where to go next in terms of your day-to-day work. Alternatively, you may be one of those people who reads the introduction and conclusion to a book to decide whether or not to invest the time in reading the rest of the book which contains the real 'meat'!

Either way, this chapter aims to draw together themes which run through the book and to illustrate those themes with reference to some of the examples used in the individual chapters. A final section considers possible future developments in the fast-moving world of educational fashion and suggests ways in which teachers can approach such initiatives with a positive outlook.

Themes running through the book

Understanding the child's perspective

Although this adage is something most teachers would probably feel that they try to achieve, it is perhaps harder than we think. Understanding how a child might perceive situations and make sense of them for themselves is a recurrent theme throughout the book. This reflects the fact that the authors, as practising educational psychologists, are constantly referring to the child's perspective, or the child's construction of events, in their everyday conversations with teachers.

Using theory to inform practice

Teachers are regularly offered a wealth of advice from a range of sources, some of which is sought and welcomed; other advice may be passed down to them unsolicited. In this context, we have tried to ensure that the content of this book is distinguishable, because it seeks to ensure that the topics addressed have psychology as their basis. We are therefore advocating that practice is not based upon pragmatic solutions 'drawn from the air' since by referring to the underlying theory in an area of focus we are more likely to derive workable and testable solutions.

The importance of context and environment

Schools and classrooms are dynamic situations where nothing happens in isolation and most events are interactional in their nature. Although we acknowledge that a class of 30 children is a class of 30 individuals, all with their own background, differences and motivations, we have sought to focus upon environmental aspects which are marginally more within the teacher's control than the personality variables and home backgrounds of the class. Therefore, although attention is given to the individual child (see Chapters 1 and 5 in particular) the emphasis in several chapters is on the context of the classroom.

Teacher as learner

Successful teachers are teachers who have enquiring minds and who are continually seeking to improve their practice. This book is aimed at such a group and throughout the book emphasis is given to the need to reflect upon practice and to learn from this. In seeking to include an individual child within a class, Chapter 1 gives suggestions of approaches that can be followed. These approaches are tools or 'props' available to the teacher but none will work unless the teacher is sensitive and reflective and willing to adjust their approach depending on the feedback they receive. This is covered in more detail in Chapter 5 where the theory of self-organised learning is described: a theory that is equally applicable to both pupils and teachers.

Including all children

The book contains some sections that apply more specifically to certain groups of children. Examples of this are given in Chapter 1 where the 'circle of friends' technique is often used with isolated children. Also, in Chapter 4 children who have experienced extreme stress or trauma are discussed and suggestions are made to aid their return to a more balanced existence.

However, by and large, the content of the book is applicable to all children and a core value, woven into each chapter, is that the psychological principles contained in the book can be applied to all children. Thus, understanding the social dynamics that affect groups is important for teachers, whatever class they are teaching. Similarly, a deeper understanding of motivational influences in children's lives is invaluable, whatever the ability level of the child.

Future developments

It is difficult to predict what lies beyond the educational horizon at any time but the pace of change over the 1990s has been unprecedented. Looking into the millennium can be a risky business! It is perhaps worth considering firstly, developments within education which have already been signalled and then secondly to look beyond education to other spheres where developments are moving ahead.

Educational trends

Schools have become familiar with the new climate of accountability where OFSTED reports and test results, in the form of league tables, are common parlance and common currency. This change in culture is set to continue with the introduction of concepts such as evidence-based teaching and 'value-added' components. Effective teaching and – of greater importance and more easily measurable – effective learning will become the focus of more detailed attention. How, then, can teachers prepare themselves for this level of scrutiny? Clearly, there is no simple answer to this question but some of the principles outlined in this book may help give direction and confidence to the beleaguered reader.

Ensuring that practice is dictated by theory and not by dogma is one clear approach that can be justified and evaluated. A demonstration that methods used have been proven to have a sound research basis means that the outcomes gained by teachers can be viewed within a wider educational context. These are principles espoused and exemplified within the book.

Beyond education

It is possible to speculate on future educational developments by examining the key changes that have occurred in other disciplines or employment contexts. Thus, education is often compared with medicine and there are certainly valuable lessons to be learned from a closer scrutiny of research and practice within the health service.

However, over the past twenty years it has often been to the business world that educational policy-makers have turned and many ideas have been imported from this area. Some of these have proved to be useful and others appear to have little applicability within an educational context. Looking to the future, management theory and in particular the management of change and the management of knowledge are key areas that could potentially be of great use within schools.

Change management is an important concept as it impacts at a variety of levels. Clearly, the pace of change within schools centres on the number of initiatives that are either required of schools, or offered to and taken on by schools. Dynamic, creative schools can be very exciting places to be but they can also be very daunting if the pace of change is unregulated.

Some head teachers are more adept at managing change than others but if the head teacher lacks essential skills the effect on individual teachers can be detrimental. An understanding of the dynamics of change and ways of dealing with it can help individuals to use change in a positive way rather than become overwhelmed by it. The development of social and communication skills alongside an understanding of organisational psychology are key areas of development where educationalists and psychologists could learn from other disciplines for the future good of the profession.

It is difficult to select particular topics as being more significant than others but a second growth area within business and organisational psychology is 'knowledge management'. This term relates to the systematic gathering, storing and retrieval of knowledge that is gained from within the work environment. Thus at the end of a particular piece of work, sophisticated I.T. is used to enable all participants to share the knowledge that they have gained from the work they have completed. With this knowledge available on networks, others can learn quickly and effectively and can adapt the new information to their particular situation.

The application of this system to schools and pedagogic practice could mean real sharing of learning; either in day-to-day teaching terms including what has worked with an individual pupil, or on a wider scale by publicising highly successful local projects where real improvement has been achieved. Aspects of this practice can be observed in the use of websites, user groups and other devices via the Internet. However, the systemisation of this knowledge within organisations takes this one step further. Reflective practice can truly be fostered and celebrated on a much wider scale than has ever been seen before.

Concluding comment

Teaching is an exciting and exacting career that requires a multitude of skills. Psychology is a dynamic, developing and infinitely-applicable discipline. The application of psychology to education is a process that reveals possibilities for real change in the lives of the individuals concerned. Enjoy it!

Appendices

Appendix 1.1
SUCCESS FOR EVERYONE
A Standard for Inclusive Educational Practice in Schools

Birmingham LEA is committed to including pupils with SEN in mainstream schools where it is in the best interests of all concerned. This document provides a framework of school improvement processes to help schools develop effective inclusive practice.

	EMERGENT	ESTABLISHED	ADVANCED
MANAGEMENT AND ORGANISATION	AWARENESS OF SEN BUDGET ISSUES	KEY STAFF, INCLUDING SENCO HAVE A BASIC UNDERSTANDING OF HOW SEN BUDGET IS CALCULATED	PLANNING PROCESS AND BUDGET DECISIONS ON SEN INVOLVE GB, SMT, SENCO. THERE ISA CLEAR UNDERSTANDING OF SEN BUDGET AND HOW IT IS CALCULATED.
	POLICIES IN PLACE, INCLUDING SEN, EQUAL OPPORTUNITIES, BEHAVIOUR, ATTENDANCE, EXCLUSIONS WHICH MEET BASIC LEGAL REQUIREMENTS OF DISABILITY DISCRIMINATION ACT	POLICIES ARE FURTHER DEVELOPED AND REVIEW IS ESTABLISHED PRACTICE	POLICIES ARE FULLY INTEGRATED IN CURRICULUM, HAVE CLEAR SUCCESS CRITERIA AND ARE REVIEWED ANNUALLY OR BIANNUALLY
	SCHOOL PROSPECTUS INCLUDES REF. TO SEN AND SENCO	H/T AND SENCO REPORTS TO GOVERNING BODY (GB)	H/T OR MANAGEMENT BODY REPORT TO GB ON PROGRESS AND IMPLEMENTATION OF POLICIES
	SENCO DESIGNATED AND TIME ALLOCATED WITH CLEAR RESPONSIBILITIES AND JOB DESCRIPTION	SENCO TAKES LEAD IN COORDINATING AND MONITORING PROVISION FOR SEN	SENCO TAKES STRATEGIC PLANNING ROLE FOR SEN PROVISION
	SCHOOL IS DISCUSSING TARGETS FOR INCLUSION	SCHOOL SETS TARGETS FOR INCLUSION IMPLICATIONS OF THE DISABILITY DISCRIMINATION ACT HAVE BEEN CONSIDERED AND SCHOOL HAS RECRUITMENT AND STAFFING PRACTICES WHICH REFLECT THE DISABILITY DISCRIMINATION ACT	SCHOOL IS REVIEWING AND EXTENDING TARGETS FOR INCLUSION DISABILITY DISCRIMINATION ACT IS EMBEDDED IN SCHOOL OBJECTIVES
	SCHOOL IS REVIEWING RECRUITMENT AND STAFFING PRACTICES IN THE CONTEXT OF THE DISABILITY DISCRIMINATION ACT		
	GOVERNANCE GB HAS NOMINATED A GOVERNOR	GOVERNANCE GOVERNORS HAVE REGULAR MEETINGS WITH SENCO	GOVERNANCE GOVERNORS ARE FULLY AWARE OF AND TRAINED IN INCLUSION ISSUES AND INVOLVED IN MONITORING WHICH INFORMS STRATEGIC PLANNING
LEADERSHIP	H/T HAS BEGUN TO DISCUSS WAYS IN WHICH SCHOOL CAN CATER FOR A WIDER RANGE OF INDIVIDUAL NEEDS	HEADTEACHER AND SENIOR MANAGERS ARE CREATING A COMMON SENSE OF PURPOSE AND ARE TOGETHER EXPLORING WAYS OF PROMOTING GREATER INCLUSION	HEADTEACHER, SENIOR MANAGERS AND GOVERNING BODY HAVE A SHARED VISION OF THE SCHOOL'S INCLUSIVE PHILOSOPHY AND PRACTICE

LEADERSHIP cont.	SENIOR MANAGERS ARE CARRYING THIS THROUGH BY EXPLORING WAYS IN WHICH SCHOOL ORGANISATION AND PRACTICE CAN CATER FOR A WIDER RANGE OF NEEDS	ALL STAFF ARE ACTIVELY EXPLORING STRATEGIES TO PROVIDE GREATER ACCESS FOR ALL PUPILS	ALL STAFF, INCLUDING ANCILLARY AND SUPPORT STAFF, SHARE THIS VISION AND ARE ACTIVELY INVOLVED IN REALISING IT IN DAY TO DAY PRACTICE
TEACHING AND LEARNING	SCHOOL DEMONSTRATES COMMITMENT TO SEN/EQUAL OPPORTUNITIES IN CURRICULUM DOCUMENTS AND SCHEMES OF WORK	ALL CURRICULUM MATERIALS AND SCHEMES OF WORK PROVIDE SOME GUIDANCE ABOUT DIFFERENTIATION	ALL SCHEMES OF WORK FULLY INCORPORATE CONSIDERATION OF A RANGE OF LEARNING NEEDS
	CURRICULUM POLICY INCLUDES REFERENCE TO SEN AT A GENERAL LEVEL	SCHOOL IS REVIEWING CURRICULUM MATERIALS/LEARNING RESOURCES TO ENSURE POSITIVE IMAGES OF SEN/LEARNING DISABILITY	ALL CURRICULUM MATERIALS/LEARNING RESOURCES ARE SELECTED OR DEVELOPED TO REFLECT POSITIVE IMAGES OF DISABILITY
	PROCEDURES ARE IN PLACE TO ENSURE EARLY IDENTIFICATION AND ASSESSMENT OF SEN	ALL CURRICULUM PLANS ADDRESS SEN AND IMPLEMENTATION IS MONITORED	
	THERE ARE SOME EXAMPLES OF CURRICULUM APPROACHES WHICH MEET A RANGE OF INDIVIDUAL NEEDS	ALL STAFF IMPLEMENT PROCEDURES FOR THE CODE OF PRACTICE	ALL STAFF IMPLEMENT AND ARE INVOLVED IN A SYSTEMATIC REVIEW OF CODE OF PRACTICE PROCEDURES
	THE NEED FOR ADDITIONAL LEARNING RESOURCES IS IDENTIFIED	SOME TEACHERS ARE DEVELOPING A VARIETY OF TEACHING AND LEARNING APPROACHES TO MEET A WIDE RANGE OF INDIVIDUAL NEEDS	ALL TEACHERS ENSURE THAT EVERY INDIVIDUAL NEED IS CATERED FOR IN TERMS OF KNOWLEDGE, UNDERSTANDING AND SKILLS
	SCHOOL HAS BEGUN TO CONSIDER WAYS TO SEEK VIEWS OF PUPIL EG CIRCLE TIME	ADDITIONAL LEARNING RESOURCES ARE TARGETED AT KEY AREAS	SCHOOL IS DEPLOYING APPROPRIATE AND SUFFICIENT RESOURCES INCLUDING STAFFING TO MEET A WIDE RANGE OF SEN
		SCHOOL HAS BEGUN TO INVOLVE PUPILS IN THEIR OWN LEARNING	SCHOOL ACTIVELY INVOLVES PUPILS IN THEIR OWN LEARNING AS WELL AS OTHER ASPECTS OF SCHOOL LIFE
ENVIRONMENT	THERE ARE SOME EXAMPLES OF DISPLAY BEING USED TO CELEBRATE A RANGE OF PUPILS WORK	STAFF AWARE OF THE NEED FOR DISPLAY FOR A RANGE OF PUPILS AND WAYS IN WHICH IT CAN BE ACHIEVED, EG THROUGH THE USE OF IT	ALL PUPILS AWARE THAT THEIR WORK IS VALUED, INDIVIDUAL ACHIEVEMENTS ARE RECOGNISED AND CELEBRATED
	ICT IS USED TO AID LEARNING THROUGHOUT THE SCHOOL	ICT IS COORDINATED TO SUPPORT LEARNING THROUGHOUT THE SCHOOL	ICT USED CONSISTENTLY AND THROUGHOUT THE SCHOOL AND EMBEDDED IN THE CURRICULUM

continued overleaf

Appendix 1.1   *continued*

	EMERGENT	ESTABLISHED	ADVANCED
ENVIRONMENT cont.	ACCESS FOR AUDIT CARRIED OUT- BEGINNING TO PLAN FOR IMPLEMENTATION, SCHOOL IS BEGINNING TO PLAN FOR ADMISSION OF PUPILS WITH A WIDER RANGE OF NEEDS THAN AT PRESENT	SOME ACCESS-AUDIT HAS BEEN CARRIED OUT AND EFFORTS HAVE BEEN MADE TO ADAPT ENVIRONMENT ENABLING MORE PUPILS TO GAIN ACCESS	ANNUAL ACCESS AUDIT CARRIED OUT – REVIEW OF ENVIRONMENT TO ENSURE THAT SCHOOL IS IMPROVING ACCESS TO MEET THE TARGETS IT IS SETTING
		REGULAR DEBATE AND AWARENESS OF INCLUSION ISSUES	TOTAL ACCESS TO THE CURRICULUM FOR A RANGE OF SEN TO ALL MEMBERS OF THE COMMUNITY
	SOME STAFF INFLUENCING GROWING AWARENESS OF ISSUES ABOUT INCLUSION	POSITIVE ATTITUDES TOWARDS SEN DEMONSTRATED ACROSS THE SCHOOL EG RESPECT FOR ALL THROUGH THE WORK OF TUTORS, ASSEMBLIES, POSTERS, RESOURCES ETC	ALL MEMBERS OF SCHOOL COMMUNITY ACTIVELY PROMOTE CLIMATE WHICH VALUES ALL SCHOOL MEMBERS
COLLECTIVE REVIEW	SOME ASPECTS OF SEN PROVISION HAVE BEEN AUDITED	TEACHERS OBSERVE EACH OTHER'S PRACTICE TO SHARE AND IMPROVE ON SPECIFIC STRATEGIES FOR SEN PUPILS	REVIEW OF PROGRESS AND ACHIEVEMENT OF SEN PUPILS INCORPORATED INTO SCHOOL REVIEW PROCEDURE
	DIFFERENCES BETWEEN GROUPS HAVE BEEN AUDITED EG BOYS, GIRLS, ETHNIC GROUPS	SCHOOL MONITORS PROGRESS OF PUPILS WITH SEN MOVEMENT OF PUPILS ON THE SEN REGISTER IS MONITORED	OTHER GROUPS MONITORED EG BOYS, ETHNIC GROUPS
			ANNUAL TARGETS SET FOR IMPROVEMENT OF PROGRESS FOR PUPILS WITH SEN SUCCESS CRITERIA WITHIN SEN POLICY
			INCLUDES EG FEWER PUPIL AT HIGHER STAGES ON SEN REGISTER
			SOME WORK DONE WITH OTHER SCHOOL EG THROUGH CULTURAL FAMILIES OF SCHOOLS
PARENTAL AND COMMUNITY INVOLVEMENT	SOME INVOLVEMENT – PARENTS ENCOURAGED TO ATTEND MEETINGS	FULLY INVOLVED IN SUPPORTING AND REVIEWING PROGRESS BUILT INTO SCHOOL PROCEDURES	MORE STRUCTURED APPROACH TO PROVIDE ROLE MODELS
	SCHOOL IS SEEKING WAYS IN WHICH PARENTS CAN BE INVOLVED	USE MADE OF ADULTS AND OTHER CHILDREN TO PROVIDE ROLE MODELS	ENVIRONMENT AND FACILITIES ARE FULLY ACCESSIBLE TO PEOPLE WITH DISABILITIES
	SENCOs REPORT TO PARENTS ABOUT PROGRESS OF PUPILS WITH SEN	SOME LINKS WITH DISABILITY GROUPS ARE BEGINNING TO BE ESTABLISHED	PARTNERSHIP WITH COMMUNITY GROUPS TO PROMOTE INCLUSION
		WIDE RANGE OF SERVICES EG LEA, HEALTH, SOCIAL SERVICES USED TO SUPPORT KNOWLEDGE, UNDERSTANDING, PROVISION IN THE SCHOOL	SCHOOL SEEKS VIEWS OF UNDER REPRESENTED GROUPS

PARENTAL AND COMMUNITY INVOLVEMENT *cont.*		SCHOOL DEMONSTRATES PRACTICAL UNDERSTANDING OF WIDE RANGE OF SUPPORT SERVICES AND HOW THEY MIGHT BE DEVELOPED KEY STAFF HAVE A WELL-DEVELOPED KNOWLEDGE ABOUT KIND OF SUPPORT THEY CAN CALL ON
STAFF DEVELOPMENT	STAFF TRAINING NEEDS FOR INCLUSION IDENTIFIED AT WHOLE SCHOOL LEVEL AND RESOURCES QUANTIFIED STAFF DEVELOPMENT PROGRAMME FOR SEN LINKED TO SCHOOL DEVELOPMENT PLAN (SDP)	THERE IS A STRUCTURED TRAINING PROGRAMME, INCLUDING INDUCTION FOR NEW STAFF, LINKED TO SDP AND INVOLVING SUPPORT SERVICES
	THERE IS AN INDUCTION PROGRAMME FOR NEW STAFF WHICH INCLUDES SEN/DISABILITY/CODE OF PRACTICE KEY STAFF, INCLUDING SEN, LEARNING SUPPORT, PASTORAL AND CURRICULUM ARE IDENTIFIED AND TRAINED	ALL STAFF, INCLUDING TEACHING AND NON-TEACHING RECEIVE TRAINING ABOUT SEN WHICH IS AUDITED AND REVIEWED REGULARLY
	SDP IDENTIFIES SEN TRAINING NEEDS ACROSS A RANGE OF DEVELOPMENT TARGETS	KEY STAFF, IE HEAD OF DEPT AND CURRICULUM LEADERS TAKE INITIATIVE
	SCHOOL HAS IDENTIFIED RESOURCES NEEDED IN ORDER TO MEET TRAINING NEEDS	SEN TRAINING NEEDS IN ALL AREAS AND FOR ALL STAFF EG PASTORAL AND CURRICULUM IDENTIFIED THROUGH SDP, RESOURCED, MONITORED AND REVIEWED ANNUALLY

Appendix 2.1
THE CLASSROOM ERGONOMICS CHECKLIST

School . . . . Room . . . .

Completed by . . . . Date . . . .

Assisted by (Staff) . . . .

        (Pupils) . . . .

I ACTIVITIES

What are the main activities to be catered for in this setting?

i)

ii)

iii)

iv)

v)

II FEATURES

	Concern	Satisfactory	Good
1 Shape of the Room	0	1	2

Floor space

Overall size and shape

Ceiling height and shape

	Concern	Satisfactory	Good
2 Windows	0	1	2

Position

Height

The view outside

Blinds or curtains

	Concern	Satisfactory	Good
3 Artificial Lighting	0	1	2

Type

Adequacy and illumination

Buzz, whine or flicker

	Concern	Satisfactory	Good
4 Heating	0	1	2

Type and position of radiators

Adequacy of temperature

Radiator noise

Radiator control

	Concern	Satisfactory	Good
5 Seating (pupil)	0	1	2

Type

Fit

	Concern	Satisfactory	Good
6 Tables (pupil)	0	1	2

Arrangement

Fit

Surface size

	Concern	Satisfactory	Good
7 Teacher Seating and Table	0	1	2

Fit

Size

Location

	Concern	Satisfactory	Good
8 Access	0	1	2

Exit/entrance doors

Emergency exits

Access to pupil storage areas

Access to staff storage areas

Access to teacher's table

Movement around the room

Access to specific equipment (e.g. sink)

	Concern	Satisfactory	Good
9 Teaching Positions	0	1	2

Talking to class/proximity of board

Teachers desk accessibility

	Concern	Satisfactory	Good
10 Flooring	0	1	2

Carpeted, tiled, wood, etc
(whole or part)

	Concern	Satisfactory	Good
11 Acoustics	0	1	2

Pupils working

Group discussion

Teacher talking

	Concern	Satisfactory	Good
12 Display	0	1	2

Notice boards

Wall space

Surface space

Book storage/display

	Concern	Satisfactory	Good
13 Storage	0	1	2

For pupils personal work

For staff

Coats

Personal belongings
(e.g. lunchbox, Games kit)

	Concern	Satisfactory	Good
14 External Distractions	0	1	2

Adjacent open plan area used by others

Adjacent corridor

Adjacent playground

Adjacent hall

Adjacent kitchens

	Concern	Satisfactory	Good
15 Computers	0	1	2

Accessibility

Visibility of screen

Suitability of seating

	Concern	Satisfactory	Good
16 Scope for Temporary Re-arrangementsfor Different Activities	0	1	2

Groupwork at tables

Individual work

Practical work

Circle time

Activity requiring floor space

III SUMMARY

Overall score   /32

Features causing concern:

Feature   Possible solution

Appendix 4.1

THE STRESS BUCKET PRO-FORMA
FOR USE IN ONE-TO-ONE INTERVIEWS
WITH A CHILD

	Stressors	In or out of own control (✓ or ✗)	Personal priority for tackling (1 –5)
Teaspoons			
Cupfuls			
Kettlefuls			

How could you improve the situation with the first three priorities that are under your control in the next six months?

(1) _____

(2) _____

(3) _____

Would this be a useful strategy for a teacher to use as a self-reflection activity as well?

Appendix 4.2

A PROBLEM-SOLVING APPROACH TO STRESS-RELATED DIFFICULTIES
(Individual or whole class)

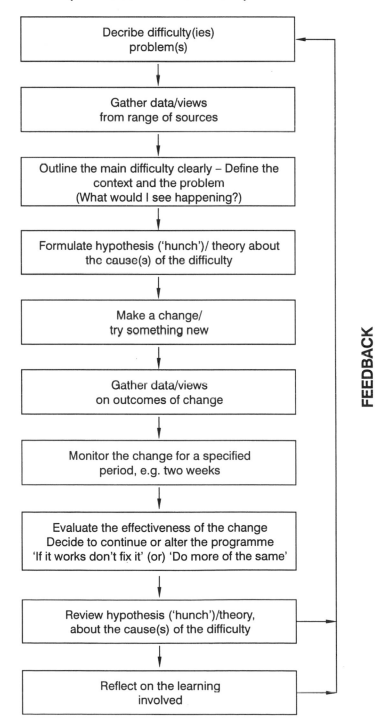

Appendix 4.3

SELF-PLANNER FOR A BETTER FUTURE
(THE I.N.S.P.I.R.E. SEQUENCE)

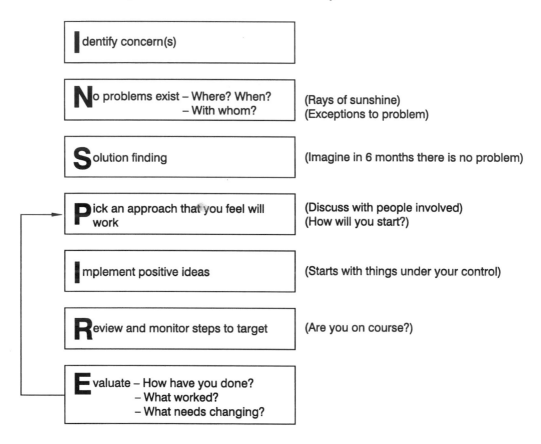

Identify concern(s)

No problems exist – Where? When?
– With whom?
(Rays of sunshine)
(Exceptions to problem)

Solution finding
(Imagine in 6 months there is no problem)

Pick an approach that you feel will work
(Discuss with people involved)
(How will you start?)

Implement positive ideas
(Starts with things under your control)

Review and monitor steps to target
(Are you on course?)

Evaluate – How have you done?
– What worked?
– What needs changing?

Appendix 4.4

CALMER PLAN SHEET

C	**C**larify what stresses are affecting you most at the moment and which ones are under your **C**ontrol (put a tick by the ones you are in control of and a cross for those that you are not)
A	**A**ssess which of the stresses that are under your control you can most easily **A**ct on (put a ring around the two that you could most easily do something about)
L	**L**ook at: What will you do differently?... .... Who/what will help you?... .... When to make the change?... .... Which lessons/situations to try it in?................................... ....
M	**M**onitor the difference How does it feel? ....
E	**E**valuate Has it worked? Who's noticed? ....
R	**R**eview Check with key person whether to continue or stop or whether to try something else? ....

Appendix 5.1

SELF ORGANISED LEARNING PRO-FORMA AND LEARNING CONVERSATION EXAMPLE

This appendix provides a pro-forma pupils can use to plan their work using the Self-Organised Learning approach. There is also a detailed example of a learning conversation-relating to Maths work in the classroom. This is provided in order to illustrate the nature of the planning and review process. Pupils will usually record their plans and reviews in much less detail than this in real life, particularly as they learn to internalise the process and move away from dependence on their coach. In the early stages of using the approach, teachers may feel it appropriate to encourage more detailed planning and recording, similar to that provided in the example, in order to ensure that pupils learn about effective planning and review. Some pupils may need to tape-record their plans and reviews because of literacy difficulties.

When introducing the approach to pupils, it will be necessary to lead them through a few planning and review cycles, attending to the detail of these processes and ensuring that each pupil understands them and has a chance to work as both coach and learner. It is important to ensure that pupils discuss benefits and any difficulties encountered in using the approach in order to learn from each other. It will also be necessary to programme time for planning and review sessions and to anticipate the need to phase out detailed recording, perhaps ending up with a simplified planning and review pro-forma based on the example given opposite.

Personal Learning Contract

Name:

What am I learning about in my plan?

My coach for this plan is:

My task is to:

My plan	What I did, what happened and what I achieved	Reasons for differences between my plan and what actually happened
My purposes for this task are:	What were my purposes?	
To achieve my purposes I will carry out these actions:	What actions did I actually carry out?	
I will know I have completed the task successfully when:	How successful was I?	
I will begin this task at … and will have completed it by …	I began the task at … and completed it at …	
My coach will review my work at …	My coach reviewed my work at …	

My strengths:	My weaknesses:

I have learned that:

Because of this in my next task like this I will:

Name: Dean Ingles.

What am I learning about in my plan? How to get better at Maths and how to work without too much talking to my friends.

My coach for this plan is: Kerry Ives.

My task is to: Complete pages 2 and 3 of the Easy-Way Maths Book to learn about adding and subtracting.

My plan	What I did, what happened and what I achieved	Reasons for differences between my plan and what actually happened
My purposes for this task are:	What were my purposes?	
1. To complete pages 2 and 3. 2. To do this quickly without talking too much. 3. To understand how to do addition and subtraction.	1. Same as planned. 2. To work quickly and to ask for help when I was stuck. (I had to talk to Carl to ask him how to do one sum. He couldn't help so I went to Mrs Ainsley. I didn't talk to anyone else.) 3. To get help with sums I don't understand. (Mrs Ainsley helped me but I still can't do some of the sums.)	1. No difference. 2. I got stuck and I needed to get help. 3. I couldn't do some of the subtraction sums.
To achieve my purposes I will carry out these actions:	What actions did I actually carry out?	
1. Write all answers down on pages 2 and 3. 2. Concentrate on my work and not talk to Carl. 3. I will work out all the answers by myself.	1. Same as plan but I didn't finish all sums. 2. I did talk to Carl and Mrs Ainsley about my work. 3. I got help to work out some of the answers.	1. I couldn't do some of sums. 2. I needed to get help when I was stuck. 3. I was stuck.
I will know I have completed the task successfully when:	How successful was I?	
1. I have finished pages 2 and 3 by 10.30 a.m. 2. I have not talked to Carl or my other friends. Mrs Ainsley will not have told me off for talking and will think I worked hard. 3. I get all the sums on pages 2 and 3 right.	1. I did not finish all of the sums in time. 2. I had to talk to ask Carl and Mrs Ainsley for help. 3. I only got 12/15 sums right and didn't finish some sums.	1. I didn't allow enough time as I needed to ask for help on some sums and had to sharpen my pencil and get my books. 2. I didn't know I would need help. 3. I couldn't do all of the sums.
I will begin this task at 10.00 a.m. and will have completed it by 10.30 a.m. My coach will review my work at 11.45 a.m.	I began the task at 10. 05 a.m. and completed it at (not finished yet) My coach reviewed my work at 3.00 p.m.	I only began working at 10.05 a.m. because I had to sharpen my pencil and get my books and Mrs Ainsley talked to me about the sums. I did other work until dinner time so did not review my work with my coach.

continued opposite

Review

$\downarrow$

My strengths:	My weaknesses:
I only talked to ask for help and I can do the additions. I was nervous about asking for help from Mrs Ainsley but I did ask her.	I couldn't do all of the subtraction sums and forgot I needed to allow time to get my books and pencils together. I could have asked Mrs Ainsley for help sooner.

$\downarrow$

I have learned that:

It's OK to talk and ask for help when I'm stuck. I need to take time to get my books and pencils together before I start work.

Because of this in my next task like this I will:

Work on the subtraction sums I still can't do. I will ask Carl or Mrs Ainsley to show me how to do them before I start work.

References

Ainscow, M. (ed.) (1991) *Effective Schools For All*. London: David Fulton Publishers.

Baker, T. and Duncan, S. (1992) *Emotional Responses to Trauma, A Developmental Perspective*. (Unpublished correspondence).

Bennett, N. (1995) 'Managing Learning Through Groupwork' in C. Desforges (ed.) *An Introduction to Teaching: Psychological Perspectives*. Oxford: Blackwell.

Bernard, M. (1994) *You Can Do It! A Motivational and Personal Development Curriculum for Increasing Student Achievement and Happiness in School and Life*. Tampa, Florida. You Can Do It! Education Inc.

Best, C. and Mead, C. (1996) 'Trauma in School. The Psychology of Helping', in Sigston, A. *et al.* (eds) *Psychology in Practice with Young People, Families and Schools*. London: David Fulton Publishers..

Bonathan, M., Edwards, G. and Leadbetter, J. (1998) *Standards for Inclusive Educational Practice*. Internal Document. Birmingham LEA.

Borich, G. and Tombari, M. (1995) *Educational Psychology: A Contemporary Approach*. New York: Harper Collins.

Bruner, J. S. (1966) *Towards a Theory of Instruction*. New York: Norton.

Burden, R. and Fraser, B. (1994) 'Examining teachers' perceptions of their working environments', *Educational Psychology in Practice*, 10(2) 67–71.

Canter, L. (1997) *Teaching Students to Get Along*. Santa Monica, California: Lee Canter Associates.

Carr, M., Kurtz, B. E., Schneider, W., Turner, L. A. and Borkowski, J. G. (1989) 'Strategy acquisition and transfer among American and German children: Environmental influences on metacognitive development', *Developmental Psychology*, 25 765–771.

Chazen, M. (1996) 'Overview Chapter', in Varma, V. (ed.) *Coping with Children in Stress*. Aldershot: Ashgate Publishing.

Cohen, L., Manion, L. and Morris, K. (1996) *A Guide to Teaching Practice* (4th edn.). London: Routledge.

Cornwall, J. and Tod, J. (1998) *Emotional and Behaviour Difficulties*. London: David Fulton Publishers.

Cox, T. (1972) 'The Nature and Management of Stress in Schools', in Clwyd County Council (ed.) Clwyd County Council, Department of Education, Conference Report, 5–29, Wales: Clwyd County Council.

Croll, P. and Hastings, N. (1996) *Effective Primary Teaching: Research-based Classroom Strategies*. London: David Fulton Publishers.

Curry, M. and Bromfield, C. (1995) *Personal and Social Education for Primary Schools Through Circle-Time*. Staffordshire: NASEN Enterprises Ltd.

D.E.S. (1967) *Children in Their Primary Schools (The Plowden Report)*. London: HMSO.

D.E.S. (1989) *Discipline in Schools: Report of the Committee of Enquiry Chaired by Lord Elton*. London: HMSO.

Daniels, H. (ed.) (1996) *An Introduction to Vygotsky*. Routledge: London.

Desforges, C. (1995) *An Introduction to Teaching: Psychological Perspectives*. Oxford: Blackwell.

Desforges, M. and Kerr, T. (1984) 'Developing Children's English in School', *Educational and Child Psychology*, 1(1) 68–80.

DfE (1994) *Code of Practice on the Identification and Assessment of Special Educational Needs*. London: HMSO.

DfEE (1997) *Excellence in Schools*. London: The Stationery Office.

DfEE (1998) *The National Literacy Strategy*. London: DfEE.

Dyregrov, A. (1993) *Grief in Children. A Handbook for Adults*. London: Jessica Kingsley Publications.

Dyson, A. (1990) 'Effective learning consultancy: a future role for special needs co-ordinators?' *Support for Learning* 5(3) 116–127.

Fisher, D. L. and Fraser, B. J. (1981) Validity and Use of My Class Inventory. Science Education 65, 145–156.

Fraser, B. J. (1986) *Classroom Environment*. London: Croom Helm.

Goleman, D. (1996) *Emotional Intelligence*. London: Bloomsbury Press.

Harri-Augstein, E. and Thomas, L. (1991) *Learning Conversations*. London: Routledge.

Harri-Augstein, E. and Webb, I. (1995) *Learning to Change*. London: McGraw-Hill.

Hastings, N. (1992) 'Questions of motivation', *Support for Learning* 7(3) 133–137.

Houghton, K. (1996) 'Working Across Boundaries', in *The D.E.C.P. Annual Course Proceedings, Educational and Child Psychology*, 13(3) 59–75.

Howarth, I. (1987) 'Psychologist and Information Technology', in Blacker, F. and Osborne, D. (eds) *Information Technology and People*: British Psychological Society.

Knight, G. and Noyes, J. (1999) 'Children's Behaviour and the Design of School Furniture', *Ergonomics* 8(5) 747–760.

Knight, G. (1999) *Classroom Ergonomics Checklist*. Unpublished. University of Birmingham.

Knight, G. R. (1994) *Junior school chairs and children's behaviour*. Unpublished MSc thesis. University of Bristol, Psychology Department.

Lazarus, R. and Folkman, S. (1984) *Stress, Appraisal and Coping*. New York: Springer.

Leadbetter, J. and Leadbetter, P. (1993) *Special Children: Meeting the Challenge in the Primary School*. London: Cassell.

Mandal (1985) *The Seated Man: Homo Sedens*. (3rd edn.). Klampenborg, Denmark: Dafnia Publications.

Markham, W. (1976) *An Introduction to Personality*. New York: Wiley.

Maslow, A. (1943) 'A Theory of Human Motivation', *Psychological Review* 50 370–396.

McCormick, C. and Pressley, M. (1997) *Educational Psychology: Learning, Instruction and Assessment*. New York: Longman.

McNamara, S. and Moreton, G. (1997) *Understanding Differentiation: A Teacher's Guide*. London: David Fulton Publishers.

Miller, A. (1991) in Lindsay, G. and Miller, A. (Eds) *Psychological Services for Primary Schools*. Essex: Longman.

Miller, A. (1996) *Pupil Behaviour and Teacher Culture*. London: Cassell.

Mischel, W. (1976) *An Introduction to Personality*. New York: Wiley.

Mortimore, P., Sammons, P., Stoll, L., Lewis, D. and Ecob, R. (1988) *School Matters*. California: The University of California Press.

National Association for Pastoral Care in Education (1993) *The Value of Pastoral Care and Personal–Social Education*. NAPCE Base: University of Warwick.

Oates, F. and Evans, (1990) 'School seating arrangements – An example of school based research in ergonomics', *Ergonomic Design of Products for the Consumer*. Proceedings of the Ergonomics Society of Australia. Adelaide, Australia 4–7 December 1990 277–282.

Pollard, A. (ed.) (1996) *Readings for Reflective Teaching in the Primary School*. London: Cassell Education.

Porter (1995) cited in Thomas, G., Walker, D. and Webb, J. (1998) *The Making of the Inclusive School*. London: Routledge.

Pugh, A. (producer) and Macrae, I. (series editor) (1995) *Old School Ties* [film]. London: BBC Disability Programmes Unit.

Salmon, P. (1988) *Psychology for Teachers*. London: Hutchinson.

Saunders, A. and Remsberg, B. (1984) *Help Your Child with Stress*. London: Piatkus.

Schein, E. H. (1990) 'Organisational Culture', *American Psychologist* 45(2) 109–119.

Shaffer, D. (1996) *Developmental Psychology: Childhood and Adolescence* (6th edn.). California: Brooks/Cole Publishing.

Solity, J. E. and Raybould, E. C. (1988) *A Teacher's Guide to Special Needs: A Positive Response to the 1981 Education Act*. Milton Keynes: Open University Press.

Stainback, S. and Stainback, W. (1996) *Inclusion; A Guide for Educators*. Baltimore: Paul Brookes Publishers.

Stanford, G. (1990) *Developing Effective Classroom Groups*. Bristol: Acorn Groups.

Stephenson, P. and Smith, D. (1987) 'Anatomy of a Playground Bully', in Tattums, D. and Lane, D. (1989) *Bullying in Schools*. Stoke-on-Trent: Trentham Books in association with the Professional Development Association.

Stoll, L. and Fink, D. (1996) *Changing our Schools*. Buckingham: Open University Press.

Szilagyi, A. D. (1983) *Organisational Behaviour and Performance*. (3rd edn). Grenview, Ill: Scott, Foresman.

Tattum, D. and Lane, D. (1989) *Bullying in Schools*. Stoke-on-Trent: Trentham Books in association with the Professional Development Association.

Taylor, J. (1997) *Furniture Plus Fitness = Healthy Attentive Pupil*. The National Back Pain Association.

Thacker, J. (1990) 'Working Through Groups in the Classroom', in Jones, N. and Frederickson, N. (eds) *Refocusing Educational Psychology*. London: Falmer.

Thomas, G., Walker, D. and Webb, J. (1992) *The Making of the Inclusive School*. London: Routledge.

Traxson, C. (1998) 'Affirmative Action – Club 2000'. *Special Children*, May 1998 27–29.

Tuckman, B. W. and Jensen, M. A. C. (1977) 'Stages of small group development revised', *Group and Organisational Studies*, 1 419–27.

UNESCO (1994) *The Salamanca Statement and Framework for Action on Special Needs Education*. Paris: UNESCO.

Vygotsky, L. (1978) *Mind in Society: The Development of Higher Psychological Processes*. Cambridge, M.A.: Harvard University Press.

Walker, D. (1995) cited in Thomas, G., Walker, D. and Webb, J. (1998) *The Making of the Inclusive School*. London: Routledge.

Wechsler, D. (1992) *Manual: Wechsler Intelligence Scale for Children* (3rd U.K. edn). London: Psychological Corporation.

Weiner, B. (1986) *An Attributional Theory of Motivation and Emotion*. New York: Springer-Verlag.

Weisaeth, L. (1993) 'Disasters: Psychological and Psychiatric Aspects', in Goldberger, L. and Breznitz, S. (eds) *Handbook of Stress: Theoretical and Clinical Aspects* (2nd edn). New York: Free Press.

West, M. (1994) *Effective Teamwork*. Leicester: British Psychological Society.

Wheldall, K. (1982) 'Seating arrangements and classroom behaviour', *Association for Child Psychology and Psychiatry News* 10 Spring 1982 2–6.

Wheldall, K. and Glynn, T. (1989) *Effective Classroom Learning: A Behavioural Interactionist Approach to Teaching*. Oxford: Basil Blackwell.

Wood, D. (1999) *How Children Think and Learn* (2nd edn). Oxford: Blackwell.

Wood, D., Bruner, J. and Ross, G. (1976) 'The role of tutoring in problem-solving', *Journal of Child Psychology and Psychiatry*. 17(2), 89–100.

Wright, A. K. *et al.* (1991) 'Investigating classroom environment in British schools', *Educational Psychology in Practice* 7(2) 100–104.

Yule, W. (1991) 'Work with Children Following Disasters', in Herbert, M. (ed.) *Clinical and Child Psychology: Social Learning*. Chichester: Wiley.